THE SCHOOL OF
HARD KNOCKS

THE SCHOOL OF HARD KNOCKS

The Evolution of Pension Investing at Eastman Kodak

Russell L. Olson

RIT CARY
GRAPHIC ARTS
PRESS

ROCHESTER, NEW YORK

To Jeanette,
my wife and best friend

The School of Hard Knocks:
The Evolution of Pension Investing at Eastman Kodak

RIT Cary Graphic Arts Press
90 Lomb Memorial Drive
Rochester, New York 14623-5604
http://wally.rit.edu/cary/carypress.html

Printed in U.S.A.
ISBN 1-933360-01-1

Library of Congress Cataloging-in-Publication Data

Olson, Russell L., 1933-
 The school of hard knocks : the evolution of pension investing at Eastman Kodak / Russell L. Olson.
   p. cm.
 Includes index.
 ISBN 1-933360-01-1
 1. Pension trusts--Investments--United States. 2. Eastman Kodak Company. I. Title.
 HD7105.45.U6O47 2005
 332.67'254--dc22
                              2005009544

Books by Russell L. Olson

The Independent Fiduciary: Investing for Pension Funds and Endowment Funds, John Wiley & Sons, Inc., 1999.

Investing in Pension Funds & Endowments: Tools and Guidelines for the New Independent Fiduciary, McGraw-Hill, 2003.

The Handbook for Investment Committee Members: How to Make Prudent Investments for Your Organization, John Wiley & Co., Inc., 2005.

Information about these books can be found at
http://www.theindependentfiduciary.com

Contents

Foreword

Throughout its 175 year history, Rochester Institute of Technology has prized and fostered learning that is application-driven. The history of RIT also happens to be closely intertwined with that of the Eastman Kodak Company through innumerable partnerships and collaborations. It thus is eminently fitting for RIT to publish Rusty Olson's insightful retrospective on Kodak's pension investments. What unfolds is an intriguing record of applied learning that lies behind a most impressive long-term financial performance.

The author played a central role in forging this record, which time and again involved applications for which no precedent existed. It is a fascinating tale, told with candor, warmth and humility, acknowledging mistakes along with the (fortunately) more dominant successes. All in all, a remarkable odyssey of learning from experience.

Thomas D. Hopkins, Dean
College of Business
Rochester Institute of Technology

Preface

Critical to the cost control and fiduciary obligations of any organization with a defined benefit pension plan is the effectiveness with which its pension fund is invested. Every dollar earned in pension investments is a dollar less* that the sponsor will have to contribute to the plan. It's that simple. But investing a pension fund well is anything but simple.

Pension plans are relatively new. Not many existed before World War II. As pension plans grew in importance during the 1950s, relatively little was known about how best to invest pension funds. This has been learned little by little over the years, and the learning process is still very much going on.

This story of Eastman Kodak Company's pension investments illustrates that learning process. I have recorded it in order to chart the progress of that learning and in the hopes that it will stimulate further learning in the years ahead about how better to invest pension assets (and endowment funds, where the principles of investing are very similar).

I have titled the book *The School of Hard Knocks* because at the outset we couldn't consult a textbook on how to invest pension assets but had to learn from the many mistakes we made. Of course, many people believe one can avoid mistakes if one avoids new approaches to investments. I have always believed that feeling bound by conventional approaches pursued by other pension funds is less than optimal, because investment theory says there are better approaches, and we should never be satisfied with anything less than the best we can achieve. Yet applying investment theory in practice often means wading into uncharted waters.

---

*Technically, every dollar earned in pension investments equates to *the present value* of a dollar less that the sponsor will have to contribute.

Fortunately, the members of Kodak's pension investment committee over the years have been open-minded enough to try uncharted waters. They have supported new ventures, recognizing that some will inevitably be disappointing. They believed that over the long term they were doing the right thing, and the long-term overall results have sustained that judgment. I have great admiration for the wisdom of those committee members, and I would like here to identify each of them from 1974 to the end of the century:

Bob Brust	Bill Love	Paul Smith
Colby Chandler	Jack McCarthy	Don Snyder
Ken Cole	Mike Morley	Virgil Stephens
Walter Fallon	Dave Pollock	Carl Stephenson
Don Fewster	Cecil Quillen	Bill Sutton
Jesse Greene	Gene Radford	Gary Van Graafeiland
Mike Hamilton	Bob Ross	Dave Vigren
Paul Holm	Bob Sherman	Gerry Zornow
Harry Kavetas	Charles Singleton	

The committee, of course, reacts to recommendations of the pension investments staff, which proposes policies and specific investment programs. The caliber of staff people with whom I have been privileged to work over the years has been truly outstanding, and I would be remiss if I didn't list their names here:

Betsy Blackburn	Peter Katsafouros	John Purves
Dick Clouser	Duff Lewis	Usha Shah
Peggy Clutz	Kat Mandel	Bob Spooner
Narvilla Coley	Dick McCarthy	Jean Tuffo
Kathleen Emert	Dave McNiff	Jim Vance
Ann Gross	Patty Pearce	Barb Veomett
Greg Gumina	Mary Jane Pocock	

I am especially indebted to my friends, Colby Chandler, Duff Lewis, John Purves, Don Snyder, and Bob Spooner, who reviewed this manuscript in draft form and provided a great many valuable suggestions. This book is much better for the effort they put into it.

I am also indebted to Eastman Kodak Company for giving me the opportunity to be a part of the learning process over the best part of three decades and, more recently, for giving me access to pension files that allowed me to verify dates and other facts.

Chapter 1

The Early Years

In 1912 Kodak founder George Eastman startled American industry by introducing an annual wage dividend for employees, with the amount tied by some formula to the dividends paid to shareholders. The wage dividend initially amounted to 2% of each employee's cumulative earnings over the previous five years. Eastman established it to give each employee "a very live interest in the prosperity of the company." He conceived it, however, not as income to be spent but as a reserve for workers' later years. But it was not an enforced savings plan. "If [employees] are extravagant and want to waste the money, the Company has no right to use any force to prevent them," he wrote.[1]

Over the next 15 years it became evident that most employees were spending their annual wage dividend, and few were saving it for retirement. A number of America's foremost companies had begun to establish pension plans, but George Eastman felt that was unnecessary at Kodak because the company already had its wage dividend plan.

A young Harvard Business School graduate by the name of Marion Folsom, who had been assistant to Mr. Eastman over the prior 10 years, felt differently. Folsom believed the right thing to do for employees was to start a pension plan, and to reduce the wage dividend accordingly to provide for its cost. In 1928 he finally convinced the aging Mr. Eastman to establish the Kodak Retirement Income Plan, or "KRIP," as it became known within Kodak.

To finance the pension plan, Folsom followed the lead of General Motors and established an "experience-rated" annuity contract with Metropolitan Life Insurance Company—Contract 34. That meant that, in return for Kodak paying Metropolitan a lump sum premium for each retiree, Metropolitan would pay that retiree a monthly pension for as long as the retiree lived. If Metropolitan earned more on its investments

---

1. Elizabeth Brayer, *George Eastman: A Biography* (Baltimore: The Johns Hopkins University Press, 1996), p. 353.

than assumed in its annuity premiums, then Metropolitan would credit dividends on Kodak's annuity contract. At the same time, Folsom negotiated with Metropolitan a minimum long-term annual interest accrual of 4%, which in 1928 Metropolitan safely assumed it could earn on its bond portfolio. In fact, as bond yields during the Depression and the ensuing war years dropped far below 4%, Folsom felt he had driven an extraordinarily good bargain for Kodak. I have often wondered what would have happened if Kodak had terminated its Metropolitan annuity contract after 20 or 25 years. Kodak might have left Metropolitan holding the bag on a deeply under-water annuity contract. As it was, Metropolitan was able to work its way back as interest rates climbed, and Kodak had to wait more than 30 years to earn its first dividend on its experience-rated contract.

Meanwhile, Marion Folsom became part of President Roosevelt's task force that designed the Social Security program during the 1930s, and after returning as Kodak's treasurer, he served in the 1950s as President Eisenhower's Secretary of Health, Education & Welfare.

Kodak's Pension Trust Fund

The Metropolitan annuity was the sole vehicle for financing Kodak's pension plan until 1960. During the 1950s many companies had begun financing their pensions through trust funds. The trust funds were irrevocably separated from corporate assets and could be used only to pay pension benefits to the pension plan's participants. At that time the trust funds were managed mainly by banks and invested substantially in U.S. common stocks. In December 1960, Kodak treasurer Don Fewster established pension trust funds with six banks—four in New York City (Morgan Guaranty, Bankers Trust, Chase Manhattan, and First National City Bank), and two in Rochester, N.Y., Kodak's home city (Lincoln Rochester Trust and Security Trust). All trust funds were invested entirely in U.S. common stocks.

Kodak continued to buy annuities on all Kodak employees as they retired (and until 1971 bought deferred annuities on many older Kodak employees), and it sent the remainder of its annual pension contributions to the six new trust funds. Fewster gave the largest portion of contributions to Morgan Guaranty and, secondly, to Bankers Trust.

Through the next dozen years, Fewster modified slightly the proportion of contributions going to each of the six banks, but he never moved any money from one trust fund to another.

About 1965 Metropolitan Life established a commingled "separate account" (separate from the participating plans' general annuity accounts) and hired an economist to invest it in U.S. common stocks so it could compete with the banks. Metropolitan then urged clients to allocate a portion of their annuity payments to that separate account, which Kodak agreed to do.

During the 1960s many companies began using independent investment managers to manage a portion of their pension trust funds, and in 1970 Kodak cautiously began doing likewise. It established a small pension trust fund with Marine Midland Trust Company in Rochester and hired the renowned T. Rowe Price to direct all investments in the fund, all in U.S. common stocks. At the same time Kodak also invested a few million pension dollars each in two common stock mutual funds—the National Growth Fund and the Windsor Fund.

Also in 1970 Fewster—perhaps excited by the fact that bond yields had reached 7%, higher than in many decades—started up another directed trust fund with Marine Midland, this one to be invested in bonds and managed internally, initially by assistant treasurer Gene Radford. That gave Kodak's overall pension trust funds (which I refer to here as "Kodak's Trust Fund") 11 different investors—six banks, one insurance company (Metropolitan), T. Rowe Price, the bond fund, and two mutual funds.

Management of pension trust funds was something with which no one at Kodak nor at most other companies at that time had any experience, so from the start it was a matter of learning from the school of hard knocks. A major study by the Ford Foundation had advocated the investment of endowment and pension assets primarily in common stocks. Over the long term, the reasoning went, common stocks gave materially better returns than bonds, and because endowment and pension funds are very long-term funds, they can withstand the high volatility of the stock market.

As a way to monitor Kodak's trust funds, Gene Radford had his secretary write on well-organized note cards every purchase and sale made by every trust fund. I was never sure what he hoped to learn from this, but the practice probably started as some sort of audit and developed a life of its own. In reviewing the portfolios of each trust fund, there was a small enough duplication of names, less than 25% in any two trust funds, that Fewster concluded that the multiple trust funds provided reasonable diversification.

Early Performance Measurement

Until 1972, Fewster had a young professional staff person, Al Kellam, calculate returns of Kodak's various trust funds. Located in a different part of the building than the main treasurer's staff, Al used a hand calculator that could do no more than multiply to do the laborious multiple-iteration job of calculating the internal rate of return since inception of each trust fund and the combined trust funds.

Periodically, Don Fewster gave a presentation about the pension trust funds at an "informational assignment" for young company executives. In it, Don included a hands-on case study. He presented, for example, the internal rate of return of each trust fund since inception through the first seven years, showed the way contributions were being allocated at that time, and asked each participant to write down what changes he or she would make in the allocation of contributions. Participants naturally would reallocate contributions on the basis of performance to date, after which Don would demonstrate how relative performance over any two years bore no resemblance to each manager's prior relative performance. It was the first inkling at Kodak of what would later become known in the investment world as the "Random Walk" syndrome.

My Initiation into Pension Investing

I joined the treasurer's staff in June 1971. I had just returned from two years at the Harvard Business School, following some 15 years in Kodak's public relations department. I had been offered a promotion to return to Kodak's public relations department but, in order to break my stereotype, I asked what else might be available. I was told about a position on the treasurer's staff, which really threw me, as I felt I knew nothing about stocks and bonds beyond an introductory course in investing the prior semester. After scratching my head for a few days, I decided to give it a try, and I quickly audited two other investment courses that last semester.

When I first joined Don Fewster's staff I had few day-to-day responsibilities. When I inquired about pension financing, Don handed me the ponderous volume of Kodak's annuity contract with Metropolitan Life and suggested I read it. It provided some of the most dense, abstruse, and sleep-inducing reading I was ever asked to do, and I learned absolutely nothing about the financial dynamics of the Metropolitan annuity contract.

Shortly thereafter I went on leave to Washington for three months to work on President Nixon's Price Commission. When I returned on April 1, 1972, I found I had been assigned to manage the bond portfolio. Since more than half of Kodak's pension assets were in annuities, which in effect were all invested in bonds, I never understood the rationale for the bond fund. Also, I felt it was unrealistic to expect me or anyone else at Kodak to do as well as a professional outside bond investor, and over the next couple of years I proved that was true.

I devoted most of my time to understanding the financial dynamics of Kodak's pension investments.

I gathered Metropolitan's annual reports on Kodak's annuity contract for the last dozen years and entered all the figures for each line item in a column so I could see the change from year to year and then tried to divine the algebra that related one column to another. This was a multi-year effort, as I made call after call to Metropolitan for explanations. I had to extract each item of information with great effort. One answer would lead, after study, to a myriad of new questions. I never could reach the bottom of the barrel. I asked how the annual dividend was calculated and was told, "It's too complicated. You'd never understand." That was like waving a red flag in front of a bull. The real answer, I eventually pried loose, was that the dividend formula was proprietary information.

Understanding the dynamics of the investment funds was seemingly a more viable challenge. Kodak's use of internal rates of return to compare managers' performance seemed inappropriate, and I wanted to introduce time-weighted rates of return. Gene Radford asked me to explain the difference to him. Time-weighted returns, I told him, allow the performance of different funds to be compared with one another and with indexes, regardless of differences in contributions and withdrawals. Internal rates of return aren't comparable, as they are dollar-weighted and therefore vary depending on each fund's particular contributions and withdrawals.

To upgrade Kodak's measurement of performance, I obtained a Monroe programmable calculator with a capacity of 512 programming steps and created a program that would calculate the present value or internal rate of return of any series of cash flows. Of course, the calculator typically took a couple of minutes or more to cough up a single internal rate of return, but it gave accurate results.

I then calculated the internal rate of return for each of our managers for every quarter since inception, and for the overall Trust Fund, then linked them through unit accounting[2] to provide time-weighted rates of return. That allowed me to establish a quarterly report to the treasurer of all 11 investment managers showing their performance for the latest quarter, the current year to date, the last 1, 3, and 5 years, and since inception. That format of performance reporting was widely used then and remains so today.

The Monroe program, which remained the department's workhorse for calculating returns well into the 1980s, also allowed me to do a study of how much predictive value there was in past performance. I compared the performance of each of our managers through a given date with their performance after that date. For example, I compared 3 years prior performance with 3 years subsequent, 5 years prior and 5 subsequent, and different combinations. I found the correlation between past and future performance was so close to zero as to make a grown man cry! On what, then, could we base decisions about managers—intuition?

---

2.   Mutual funds use unit accounting to update each fund's share price (its unit value) by its percentage price change every day. Rates of return calculated from these prices (unit values) are *time-weighted* rates of return. Pension portfolios are typically valued only at the end of every month or quarter. A portfolio's internal rate of return (dollar-weighted rate of return) is calculated each quarter, for example, and then the portfolio's unit value is updated by that quarterly return. Time-weighted rates of return can be calculated from these unit values.

Muddling Through the 1973–74 Market Crash

The year 1971 was a great year for the Trust Fund. Its 21% return was 7 points better than the return on Standard and Poor's 500 index. The following year the Trust Fund matched the S&P 500's 19% return. Each year I drafted Gene Radford's favorable slide presentation to senior management.

Then came 1973. The S&P 500 was down 15%, and the Kodak Trust Fund was down 20%. After I prepared Gene Radford's presentation to senior management, he turned to me and said, "Rusty, you prepared the report. Why don't you give it." So I bore the bad news.

In 1974, the S&P 500 plummeted another 26%, and Kodak's Trust Fund matched it. Again, I related the bad news to senior management—Kodak chairman Gerry Zornow, CEO Walter Fallon, and CFO Bob Sherman. Total Trust Fund assets, which had equaled $500 million at the end of 1972, almost the same as our annuity assets, had dropped to $378 million after 1974, despite some $110 million in new contributions. The time-weighted rate of return for the 14 years since inception was less than 3%. Remarkably, no one questioned why we had gotten into risky investments like common stocks in the first place.

Meanwhile, Don Fewster had retired and Gene Radford had succeeded him as treasurer. I was given the title of assistant to the treasurer, pension investments and shareholder services, which meant I also supervised Kodak's stock transfer agent and responded to all letters from shareholders about their accounts.

Our First Manager Termination

In 1974 Gene Radford and I agreed to recommend for the first time firing a Kodak fund manager. When the Windsor mutual fund was added late in 1970, it was viewed as a conservative fund that would serve as a bulwark against a down market. But it was a major disappointment. It greatly underperformed in 1971–72 when the market was very strong, and then it performed 10 percentage points *worse* than the terrible return on the S&P 500 in 1973. That's all we needed to know—out with the Windsor Fund!

We reviewed which mutual funds had been some of the more successful throughout this era, and one was the high-quality Chemical

Fund, which had outperformed the S&P 500 by 4 points per year over the prior eight years. What an attractive swap! Subsequently, we sold the Chemical Fund and hired its manager, the Eberstadt organization, to manage a larger, direct account.

That was the era of the Nifty Fifty "one-decision" stocks. Some 50 of the larger stocks that had consistent growth in earnings—such as IBM, Kodak, and Avon—were bid up to price/earnings ratios of 40 or 50. Meanwhile, investors shunned small stocks, cyclical stocks, and higher-yielding but slower-growing stocks.

About the time we were selling the Windsor Fund, I understand that its manager, John Neff, was overwhelmed with frustration. John had gained fame for his selection of value stocks, but now he went to his management at Wellington Management Company and said they should probably replace him, as everything he touched seemed to turn to dust. His boss asked him, "John, what have you been doing differently?"

"Nothing!" John replied.

"Then hang in there, John, and keep doing it," came the response.

We had never visited John Neff. We hadn't even talked with him on the telephone. In truth, we didn't understand his investment style nor even how different sectors of the market were performing. If we had done our homework really well, would we still have sold the Windsor Fund? Of course, we'll never know, but we'd have been in a far better position to make an informed decision.

As it was, the Windsor Fund outperformed the Chemical Fund by 20 percentage points *per year* over the next four years and then by 8 points per year for the subsequent seven years. By 1984 the Chemical Fund's manager, Eberstadt, was merged out of existence.

Our Weak Rebound

The stock market did bounce back strongly in 1975, as the S&P 500 was up 37%. Yet Kodak's Trust Fund managed only 26%. And the following year when the S&P was up another 24%, the Trust Fund achieved only 15%. Then in 1977 when the S&P declined by 7%, the Trust Fund was down 8%.

CEO Walter Fallon wrung his hands and asked, "Why can't we

get investment managers we can trust—like Roger Anderson" (Kodak board member who was chairman of Continental Illinois Bank in Chicago). Fortuitously, I had been tracking the performance of large banks and sent up to Walter that same day a copy of Continental Illinois's performance. I never heard another such word from Walter.

Meanwhile, we made a couple of other changes. We hired two venerable investment management firms in Boston, Putnam and State Street Research & Management, to replace Rochester's Security Trust Company, Metropolitan's separate account, First National City Bank, and the bond fund.

Termination of our bond fund was consistent with our mentality that Kodak's Trust Fund should be 100% equity oriented. Throughout the 1970s, that mentality reflected the fact that the value of Kodak's annuities—in effect, the most conservative of fixed-income investments—was greater than that of Kodak's Trust Fund. That mentality—of being 100% equity oriented—remained into the late 1980s, when the value of Kodak's annuity general-accounts assets finally dropped below 10% of total KRIP assets. Over time, however our definition of "equity" stretched to include any asset class whose expected returns equaled or exceeded those on common stocks.

In selecting new managers, we at least didn't make the mistake of hiring the managers with the best records during the 1973–74 market crash. There were two managers who miraculously went into cash early in 1973 and were absolute heroes! But they didn't get back into stocks in time for the abrupt market run-ups in 1975 and 1976, and by the end of the decade no one remembered them.

Most of our bank managers charged an annual fee of about 0.25% of their account's market value, and that covered trust services as well as investment management. Independent investment managers, such as T. Rowe Price, Putnam, or State Street charged somewhat more, but many who called on us charged fees of 0.50% or higher, which we considered exorbitant. I later learned that while we were paying low fees we were getting just what we paid for.[3]

---

3.   By 1979 total KRIP management and trustee fees—always paid directly out of KRIP assets—amounted to 0.36% of KRIP assets. Fees reached a high of about 0.75% of assets in 1994, leveling off at about 0.60% by the end of the decade.

By the end of 1977 Kodak's Trust Fund had returned only 4.2% per year since its 1961 inception and had underperformed the S&P 500 by more than 2% per year. Surprisingly, the A.G. Becker report[4] indicated that over half of all U.S. pension funds had performed even worse over most intervals, possibly because the other funds included a sizable allocation to bond accounts. Few of the other pension plans used annuities.

The concept of an index fund seemed a sound one, and in 1977 Kodak's was one of the first pension funds to invest in an index fund—one managed by American National Bank of Chicago to replicate the S&P 500. Its fees were eventually less than 0.02% per year. Initially, managers of index funds felt it their fiduciary duty to avoid the relatively small number of stocks in the index that were in the poorest financial condition. We didn't want our manager to avoid those stocks, however, as once those stocks were identified, they had, over time, outperformed the index.

ERISA

In 1974 Congress passed the Employee Retirement Income Security Act (ERISA) to ensure that companies were funding and investing their pension plans properly so plan participants could be assured of receiving the pensions they were promised. A key provision of ERISA laid down strict new fiduciary standards for the operation of private pension plans. ERISA provided that overall fiduciary responsibility for managing a pension plan must rest with a "named fiduciary." A company's board of directors became the "named fiduciary" of the company's pension plans unless the board appointed one or more persons to fill that role. Kodak's board appointed a committee, and hence was born "KRIPCO"—the Kodak Retirement Income Plan Committee, consisting of Kodak's chairman, president, CFO, treasurer, and director of compensation and benefits. Hence there was no great change in the particular persons to whom our pension investment program reported.

---

4.   A.G. Becker was a brokerage firm that by the early 1970s had become the most widely used provider of performance measurement to U.S. pension funds, a service that about 1984 was sold to SEI.

Another change driven by ERISA was Kodak's 1976 addition to the company's legal staff of an ERISA attorney, John Purves, to work with KRIPCO and the investment staff. John was a key member of the team for the next 21 years. John emphasized that the members of KRIPCO are individually responsible for investment policy and all other committee decisions, which means they can be sued as individuals for any decision that violates that fiduciary responsibility.

John prepared KRIPCO meeting agendas and minutes with as much care as a corporate secretary prepares agendas and minutes for boards of directors. And whenever staff considered a recommendation, we always had to review it with John beforehand. John reviewed carefully even the simplest recommendation to be sure that neither the recommendation nor the wording of its supporting arguments could be viewed as questionable under ERISA. He also made sure we retained appropriate documentation in a permanent file. If the recommendation was for an unusual investment or a limited partnership, John would spend a great deal of effort ensuring that it met the prudence requirements of ERISA, sometimes even hiring outside counsel to confer with him. John's tedious procedure was often both time-consuming and irritating for staff. Our appreciation for John's stickler reviews, however, zoomed way up in 1994 when Kodak sailed through an in-depth review of KRIP by the U.S. Department of Labor.

John's careful process allowed KRIP ultimately to enter with confidence many investments that a lot of other pension investment staffs wouldn't even discuss with their committees. John's biggest challenge was to help structure what he considered these cutting-edge investments. His mindset with each investment opportunity was: "If anything goes wrong, how do I defend our action?" Under the new law there was little or no precedent, but he determined he could defend an investment if we followed certain steps and procedures founded on thorough research and logic.

A major change occurred in 1983, when membership in KRIPCO was re-constituted, to consist of the CFO as chairman, plus the treasurer, vp/general counsel, vp for human relations, and director of wage and salary. That composition remained largely intact through the end of the century, although at times KRIPCO expanded to include two retirees who were former KRIPCO members. Also in the early 1980s, the treasurer began meeting each summer with the finance committee of the board of directors to report on investment results of the pension plan.

As our staff recommended manager changes, I made the presentations to KRIPCO, but—in the 1970s—only after Gene Radford and I had both met with each prospective manager, and only after we had reviewed our proposals in advance with CFO Bob Sherman. Bob told us what he thought could or could not be gotten through CEO Walter Fallon. If the proposal was borderline, Sherman would try to pre-sell the idea to Fallon before the meeting.

At virtually no time did any of our managers or prospective managers meet with KRIPCO (except a certain few of them who later participated in KRIPCO's off-site pension conferences). Not only would the committee's meeting with each manager be unwieldy, given the number of managers we had, but everyone agreed it would also be useless. In a 20- or 30-minute presentation to a committee, the only thing committee members can do is determine which manager is more articulate, and we all recognized there is essentially no correlation between articulateness and investment management capability.

When in 1975 Gene Radford and I first recommended a new manager, we developed three finalist candidates and presented all three to KRIPCO for the committee to choose among them. On our next presentation, newly elected president Colby Chandler said, "Why do you ask us to decide among them? You've done all the research. You're in a much better position to decide. Which one do you recommend?" That was the last time we ever presented a choice of new managers. Colby Chandler's wisdom remains impeccable, as his approach holds staff properly accountable.

The Performance Triangle

From the start, I searched with high priority for the most helpful way to portray a manager's past performance. The typical graphs provided by managers weren't of much help. Also inadequate for analysis was our Trust Fund's quarterly performance format that showed results over the last 1, 3 and 5 years and since inception. After trying many formats,

I finally—around 1976 or 1977—hit upon a format that became our standard analytical tool for the next 25 years: the performance triangle. Exhibit 1 (on the next page) illustrates the triangle with an arbitrarily selected mutual fund. The triangle also became our standard way to portray a manager's performance before our committee.

The triangle compares the manager's performance, net of fees, with its benchmark over every interval of years. (Of course, at the time, the S&P 500 was the only benchmark we used.) The advantage of the triangle is that it prevented us from looking at short-term performance without seeing it in the context of long-term performance. The triangle showed the manager's consistency. We discovered that virtually every good manager has intervals of years when he underperforms his benchmark. Conversely, nearly every poor manager has intervals of relative success. By noting intervals when each manager outperformed or underperformed his benchmark, and by recalling the nature of the market in those years, we could gain a quick insight into the manager's style and could develop a series of useful questions to probe further into the manager's approach.

Analyses of Portfolio Composition

Also during the late 1970s we subscribed to an analytical service from a New York investment house, Faulkner Dawkins. We submitted to them the portfolio of each of our managers at the end of a quarter, and they provided us a composition analysis of each of the portfolios and of our composite Trust Fund. They programmed it to my idiosyncratic requirements—weighted medians and quartiles (which are much more helpful than averages) for price/earnings and price/book ratios, volatility of earnings, return on equity, and market cap. They also calculated the portfolio's dividend yield and the percentage breakdown of the portfolio by industry. For the first time, we began to understand the differences among our managers.

Exhibit 1

Illustration of Performance Triangle

Vanguard Primecap Fund vs. S&P 500 Index

--------------------------------From Start of--------------------------------

	'89	'90	'91	'92	'93	'94	'95	'96	'97	'98	'99	'00	'01	'02
To end of '02	3	3	4	4	4	4	3	3	4	4	6	3	-2	-2
'01	4	4	4	5	5	5	4	5	6	7	10	6	-1	
'00	4	5	5	6	6	6	5	6	9	11	17	14		
'99	3	4	4	4	5	4	3	4	7	8	20			
'98	2	2	2	2	2	1	-2	-2	0	-3				
'97	2	3	3	3	3	2	-1	-1	3					
'96	2	2	3	3	3	2	-3	-5						
'95	3	4	4	5	6	5	-2							
'94	4	4	6	6	9	10								
'93	3	3	4	5	8									
'92	1	1	2	1										
'91	1	1	3											
'90	1	0												
'89	1													
Actual for Year	32	-3	33	9	18	11	35	18	37	25	41	4	-13	-25

White = Outperformed Benchmark

Gray = Underperformed Benchmark

The bottom line, "Actual for Year," shows the actual total return on the Primecap Fund for each particular year.

All figures in the triangle are *relative*—the Primecap Fund's total annual return for that interval *minus* the total annual return on its benchmark, the S&P 500.

For example,

The hypotenuse shows the Primecap Fund's return for each induvidual year relative to the S&P 500.

The figure "3" in the upper left-hand corner means that the Primecap Fund outperformed the S&P 500 by 3% per year for the 14 years 1989–2002.

The gray "-2" from the start of 1995 to the end of 1998 means the Primecap Fund underperformed the S&P 500 by 2% per year for that 4-year interval.

Meeting with Investment Managers

It was the custom in the 1970s for a manager to meet with each client once each quarter to review the quarterly performance and the outlook. From the start, I began asking myself why I seemed to gain so little from those quarterly meetings. The reasons were twofold. First, the dissection of the quarter's performance was extremely myopic even though the greatest determinant of short-term performance is market noise. And second, the manager's comments and forecast for the economy were not only useless but had nothing material to do with how he managed our portfolio. In short, we learned little about what distinguished his management approach from that of other managers.

Accordingly, we planned only a single meeting a year on the basis that that was a better use of everyone's time. We held the majority of these meetings in the managers' own offices, where we could meet with more of their people. Certainly, a manager could make more money for us by managing our portfolio than by holding our hand. But our annual meetings with managers evolved into thoroughly pre-planned affairs. Prior to each meeting we studied the manager's performance triangle and analyzed his portfolio composition. We also began sending each manager a questionnaire a month or two prior to the meeting under the principle that we should know as much about our existing managers as we did about a prospective new manager. Moreover, the questionnaire took care of objective data in an efficient manner, and we could focus the meeting on subjective questions that we developed from our analyses and from the manager's questionnaire response. This time-consuming procedure remained the staff's disciplined approach into the new century.

Of course, we always met additionally with our investment managers whenever they or we felt that a special meeting would be helpful.

A Master Trustee

Throughout this time, we still received 11 different trust reports each month, each with a different format, and we had to laboriously compile all the data to see how our overall Trust Fund was doing. We knew life would be far simpler if we had only a single master trust fund. Many banks tried to sell us their master trust services, but I could not see for a long time how we could justify the added expense. Finally, we decided we could swing it if we told our bank managers we would reduce their annual fees by 0.04% when we switched them from managing their own trust fund to managing a directed account in our master trust. We took the chance that none of our managers would terminate our account (none did).

Doing a study on master trust candidates in 1978 was one of the most extensive research jobs I ever did. I prepared an extremely long questionnaire and sent it to Bankers Trust, Chase, and Citibank in New York City, State Street Bank in Boston, Marine Midland in Rochester, Mellon Bank in Pittsburgh, Northern Trust in Chicago, and Boston Safe Deposit and Trust Company. I then compiled their responses to each question side by side and wound up with a huge analytical stack. Citibank and Boston Safe appeared to provide the best value for the money. Citibank was far better known. Boston Safe's only major pension client was Mountain States Bell. But Boston Safe more readily agreed to do special programming for us to provide accrual accounting (far from standard in the industry then, but required at yearend by Kodak's auditors), and to provide the kind of portfolio composition analyses we had been getting from Faulkner Dawkins. Also, Boston Safe would have every staff person assigned to our account in a single office, whereas Citibank distributed different trustee functions among several different departments. We liked dealing with a single coordinated staff. (This changed many years later, but Boston Safe was still able to maintain a high quality of service.)

Our choice of Boston Safe created much buzzing on Wall Street. An executive of State Street Bank was quoted as saying, "I never realized Kodak was such a high flyer as to choose 'Boston Who?!'"

Our choice proved most fortuitous, as Boston Safe gave us consistently solid performance through the years. The staff members it assigned to the Kodak account were, with very few exceptions, well-qualified people who really cared. Perhaps the best part of the relationship is that many times we asked Boston Safe to do things it had never thought of doing before. Sometimes, it didn't do them as fast as we might have liked, but it never said no. It always figured out a way to do them, and well. Boston Safe was purchased by Mellon Trust in the early 1990s, but the Boston Safe operation remained intact in Boston and continued to provide good service.

An example of the new challenges we threw at Boston Safe occurred in 1989 when we hired Emerging Markets Management to invest in stocks of Third World countries. Boston Safe had to scramble to find competent sub-custodians in each of the countries, and it got off to a bumpy start. The people at Emerging Markets Management complained about having to do too much hand-holding. Yet two years later, when Emerging Markets Management started up a mutual fund, whom did it choose as custodian? Boston Safe.

Moving to a master trustee at the beginning of 1979 was one of the most important moves we ever made. Without a competent master trustee, we could not possibly have done the many useful, complex things we did over the next 20+ years.

The Start of Real Estate Investments

In the early 1970s Prudential and then Equitable had started up commingled separate accounts to invest in commercial real estate—office buildings, shopping centers, warehouses, and apartments. Pension funds could go in or out of those funds each month on the basis of unit values, which were based on appraised values of properties. Each property was appraised by an outside appraiser once a year, and the insurance company's staff estimated interim changes in appraisals to maintain what was deemed a fair unit value.

Intuitively, it seemed to me that an ideal way to run a pension fund was to have multiple kinds of investments that marched to different drummers, although I had not the faintest idea how one could ever achieve that. Real estate, however, seemed like an excellent diversifier, and I began keeping track of the quarterly results of the Prudential and Equitable funds. Returns were not great, except by comparison with returns on the stock and bond markets, which had been poor.

When I suggested we consider seriously those two real estate funds, KRIPCO was not interested in hearing about it. Until, that is, one day early in 1979 when CFO Bob Sherman came back from an Aetna board meeting announcing that he had just learned of the best thing since sliced bread—a commingled real estate separate account that Aetna was starting up. I quickly dusted off my up-to-date data on the Prudential and Equitable funds, and very soon KRIP had taken a small piece of all three.

At the same time, we were visited by what seemed like a more entrepreneurial team from San Francisco—the Rosenberg Real Estate Equity Fund (RREEF). Unlike the insurance company funds, RREEFs were closed-end funds to which investors would make commitments. RREEF would then take down cash from investors whenever it needed the money to buy properties, and it promised to sell the properties after 10 years. Because RREEF's managers seemed more entrepreneurial, we also convinced KRIPCO to make commitments to two RREEF funds in 1979.

Chapter 2

The Turning Point

During the summer of 1978 CFO Bob Sherman suggested to treasurer Gene Radford and me that it might be useful to have a consultant make a one-time review of our pension investment program and give us his evaluation and recommendations. Gene and I flew to Tacoma, Washington, to visit the best-known consultant, Frank Russell & Company. We were greeted warmly by CEO George Russell and were treated to a gourmet dinner on his yacht in Tacoma Sound. Russell, however, was not interested in doing a one-time assignment. He wanted instead to become an ongoing consultant at an annual six-figure fee. That was not what we had in mind.

I asked each of our managers which consultants asked them the most insightful questions, and the name I kept hearing was the relatively new firm of Rogers, Casey & Barksdale in Stamford, CT. We met in November with Steve Rogers and John Casey, and they seemed pleased to do the review.

Steve and John endorsed our decisionmaking hierarchy (with KRIPCO) and rated our information database and search process as very thorough, but Steve insisted we needed to put "discipline" into our process. With our analytical and other processes, I thought we *had* a disciplined approach! But that's not what he meant. Steve showed us that our managers were so similar in approach that our multiple managers were giving us very little diversification. All were investing overwhelmingly in large U.S. stocks, all with some form of a growth bias. Each of our managers, he maintained, should serve a complementary niche. He was basically saying we should make a major change in our investment manager batting lineup.

Early in 1979 we reported to KRIPCO results of a study of the performance of 166 commingled common stock funds for 1974–78.

Of these 166 funds, bank-managed funds accounted for:

> None of the top 20%
> 9% of the second quintile
> 21% of the third quintile
> 24% of the fourth quintile
> 46% of the bottom quintile

We added that results were not greatly different for other 5-year intervals, and we surmised that the best investment managers seem to be attracted away from banks.

Revised Investment Structure

Working with Rogers and Casey, I proposed in May 1979 a revised investment structure for Kodak's Trust Fund, which since the beginning of that year had become a single master trust. By then, Don Snyder had succeeded Gene Radford as treasurer of Kodak, but Don gave me continued strong support. Excerpts from the 16-page single-spaced document include:

> **Importance.**
> Every *1% per year* in the performance of the Trust Fund (not including annuities) equates to $10 million in [the present value of] Kodak's pension contributions—perhaps $20 million by 1983, the way our Trust Fund is likely to grow....

> **Why common stocks?**
> Despite underperformance in recent years, common stocks have still outperformed U.S. Treasury bonds by 5% per year for the 53 years 1926–78 [based on the recent Ibbotson-Sinquefield study].... Stocks must provide better returns over the long term if our economic system is to survive. Otherwise, no rational investor will risk equity capital, which is a sine qua non of our economy.... Kodak is in a position to take the long view and invest in whatever will reduce Kodak's pension costs long term.

Why not buy stocks only in good markets?
Ideally a trust fund manager should move back and forth from cash to bonds to stocks (time the market) depending on when stocks are favorably priced. We know managers who have done this at times. *But we know none* who has demonstrated it can do so consistently. *Nor have consultants* been able to identify such managers.

Trust Fund objectives:
> *Aggregate long-term performance*—To exceed the total return of the stock market (as measured by the S&P 500) and to place in the top quartile of the nation's pension funds in equity performance.
> *Aggregate volatility constraint*—To incur no more volatility than the stock market average, as measured by the standard deviation from long-term average performance.

The S&P 500 is tough to beat.
For all participants, the stock market is less than a zero-sum game: The average participant must underperform the market by the costs of transactions and management. Even managers with the best long-term records have underperformed the market over intervals as long as three to five years.

This led us to establish our Index Fund two years ago [in 1977].... Our Index Fund has since proved it can do the job well and inexpensively. It can be expected to provide above average performance (relative to other pension funds) and, at times, first quartile performance.

Recommendation.
In order to lock up the market returns with a good part of our trust fund, we recommend:
> Establish a *Part C* (Core) of our Trust Fund, amounting to about 60% of the fund (not including real estate). Invest Part C in index-type funds.

Part C will provide a bulwark for our common stock investment program. By definition, Part C would always be fully
invested in common stocks.

Place the remainder of our Trust Fund (not including real
estate) in *Part P* (Performance)—among a group of common
stock managers who

   a) have proven records of superior performance,
   b) concentrate on the style or sector of the market they
      know best, and
   c) complement one another in their styles and market
      sectors so that their aggregate volatility is not greater
      than the overall stock market. The performance goal
      of Part P should be 1.5 percentage points [per year]
      higher than the S&P 500 return....

Under this approach, managers should not act, as they do now,
as if each is managing all our common stocks. We must indi-
vidualize our objectives to each manager, comparing its performance—where feasible—against the particular segment of the
market in which it specializes.

Few banks will probably qualify for this role, except in particular areas of expertise. Large banks have generally not been
able to equal the performance of the S&P 500.

Real Estate.
Entry into real estate equity funds was approved by KRIPCO
March 28 [1979]. In due course, we would move up to 5% of our
total pension assets into real estate.

Although long-term performance is not expected to equal
common stocks, real estate equities should provide three
advantages:

   a) Total returns should be better than bonds. (We estimate
      11% per year, which real estate funds have achieved over
      the last five years.)
   b) Volatility appears to be dramatically less than stocks
      and even less than bonds.
   c) In times of accelerating inflation, real estate assets
      have provided the best inflation protection.

No change in existing policy:
Whenever an employee retires or terminates with a vested right to pension benefits, the Company purchases an annuity for that person so it is thereafter the obligation of a life insurance company to make promised pension payments to him.

Projected allocation of assets.
Assuming stock market returns average 13% over the next four years, our asset mix could change by 1982 to about 38% in annuities, 5% in real estate, and 57% in common stock and cash. [The assumption of 13% total return hinged on a projected price/earnings ratio for the stock market of 8.5 in 1982.]

Implementation.
Approve this proposed policy statement in June [1979]. Then:
- Terminate Bankers Trust [over $100 million] and Lincoln First [nearly $100 million].
  [Chase Manhattan had already been terminated.]
- Reconsider Morgan's direct holdings. [We removed some 90% of assets from Morgan Guaranty's account, leaving only about $15 million in its commingled international common stock fund.]
- Hire Neuberger & Berman. [We moved about $50 million into Neuberger & Berman—the maximum Neuberger would take initially—and the rest into our index fund.]

Longer term:
- Re-evaluate T. Rowe Price and Eberstadt. Do they add value?
- Should we pursue international investments? If so, who, how much, and when?
- Search for additional Part P managers whose members complement one another well.

One might consider the recommendation to terminate Lincoln First (a Rochester bank) and to remove most of the assets from Morgan Guaranty rather naïve, as CEO Walter Fallon was a member of Morgan Guaranty's board of directors, and CFO Bob Sherman a director of Lincoln First. I blithely assumed that the facts were clear enough that

KRIPCO would approve the recommendations.... and it did! Bob Sherman simply asked me to defer telling our investment manager at Lincoln First until he had personally been able to tell the CEO of Lincoln First—an appropriate request.

Informing an investment manager that we were terminating his account was one of the most distasteful tasks that went with my job. I virtually always made it a point to visit the terminated manager and tell him the bad news in person. The case of Lincoln First was especially awkward. The head of Lincoln's investment department had been new to Rochester three years before and I had befriended him and successfully encouraged him and his family to join the church where my family and I were members. He could see how badly I felt about giving him the news, and I will never forget his response. Disappointed as he was, he said, "If friends can't part company when they should, then friends shouldn't do business together in the first place." What class!

The Neuberger Story

The hiring of Neuberger proved a far-reaching event. Because my flight to New York City in the spring of 1979 landed early, I arrived on my initial visit to Neuberger's Fifth Avenue office before 8 o'clock. At that hour its office was quite empty, except for one person sitting at a Quotron in the war room whom I recognized from his picture to be the renowned founder Roy Neuberger himself. Roy had created the Guardian mutual fund in 1950 and personally managed it to a superb performance record over the next 27 years.

When my discussions with Neuberger's client service director became serious, he turned to me and carefully said, "I'd like to ask you a question and would appreciate a frank answer. Roy Neuberger, now 76 years old, gave up managing the Guardian Fund two years ago so we could retain a great but ambitious young manager. Since then, Roy's been like a kid who's lost his toys. He's been kind of a nuisance getting into the business of all our other investment managers. How would you like to have Roy personally manage your account?"

I quickly replied yes, and KRIPCO backed me up. It was one of our best decisions. Roy managed our account for nine years, compounding 19% per year, 3 percentage points better than the S&P 500, and better than the average Neuberger manager achieved. In 1984, in order to let us continue to benefit from Roy's stock-picking ability, we authorized Roy to sell S&P 500 futures when he was bearish on the market instead of building up cash, as he had occasionally done. For most of 1987 Roy sold index futures, as he thought the market had become overvalued, and for much of the year he groused within the Neuberger shop because most of the firm's other managers were performing better than he. Then along came October 1987, when the market plummeted 25%. When the price of the index futures was close to bottom, Roy bought them all back and finished the year up 15%, better than other Neuberger managers (as usual).

In 1988 Roy quit "while he was still ahead." He was about to turn 85. For more than a dozen years thereafter he was still in his office every day trading his own stocks, and he continued to be a good friend and important adviser to the Kodak fund. In the summer of 2003 I attended Roy's 100th birthday party, at which time he was still trading stocks from his own apartment.

The Value Line Story

The head of American National Bank of Chicago's investment department was Rex Sinquefield, who with Roger Ibbotson had done the seminal study of stock and bond returns going back to 1926. Rex impressed on me how small stocks, the smallest 10% listed on the New York Stock Exchange, had achieved a couple of percentage points per year better performance over the years than the S&P 500. Small stocks were very volatile, but they had only a modest correlation with the S&P 500. I calculated that a portfolio composed 80% of the S&P 500 and 20% of such small stocks (rebalanced annually) would over the years have achieved a higher return than the S&P 500 alone, but with a *lower* volatility (because of the modest correlation). Hence, we set out looking for a great manager of small stocks.

We wound up in New York City in 1980 meeting with Value Line, which was (and is) noted for its weekly stock guide in which it ranked 1,700 stocks, and we talked with Sam Eisenstadt, who developed the ranking system. Sam had just developed a different ranking system expressly designed to rank a couple of thousand small stocks, and Value

Line was looking for a client for whom it could manage a portfolio based on that new ranking system. The simulated returns on the new system were truly exciting. That, combined with the demonstrated success of Value Line's published ranking system, convinced us to place some $80 million with Value Line as its first small-stock client.

Before hiring Value Line, we got its senior managers to agree they would never accept more than $X million dollars (or more than Y% of the total capitalization of all small-cap stocks). Even though we were Value Line's first client for this program, we were concerned, if they were successful, that they might impair their ability to achieve great returns by taking on too much money to manage. This became a standard procedure for us in hiring small stock managers, and Value Line—like most other small-stock managers we hired—stuck conscientiously to our agreement. One small-stock manager we hired in the early 1990s exceeded the limit he had agreed to, and we terminated the account less than nine months after hiring him.

Value Line's returns in its first couple of years were so good that I had to deter members of KRIPCO from allocating a lot more assets to Value Line at the top of the small-stock market. Over the next 17 years, through a series of account managers and considerable turnover in its team of young analysts who were assigned full time to our account, Value Line outperformed the Russell 2000 small-stock index by some 2½ percentage points per year (net of fees).

"Selling the Losers" and Other Losers

Also in 1981 we started up a second, small account with Value Line, which we called our "Sell The Losers" account. Of its published rankings, Value Line's bottom-10%-ranked stocks had a marvelous record of underperforming the S&P 500. Why not have Value Line sell the losers out of American National's index fund? We instructed our trustee, Boston Safe, to make available to Value Line our index fund holdings, from which Value Line could sell those it considered losers without American National ever knowing it. Value Line, of course, could buy back only the stocks that were in its negative portfolio.

What a challenge for our trustee, Boston Safe: Portfolio A would be what American National *thought* it held. Portfolio B would be the stocks Value Line had sold—a *negative* portfolio. And Portfolio C would be A minus B—the actual stocks held in our index fund. Somehow, Boston Safe managed to do it.

How did that work out? We ran the program for half a dozen years and in 1987 terminated it with a net loss of $6 million. Why didn't it fly? Partly, I believe, because Value Line couldn't transact a stock until it had published its ranking. Partly because of transaction costs. And partly ... I really don't know.

Selling the Losers wasn't the only new program we tried that ended in a loss. For example, in 1983 we hired a California manager for the sole purpose of selling call options on any stocks in our aggregate portfolio. If a stock was subsequently called, the manager had to meet the call by buying the stock on the open market. That program ended in early 1989 with a small cumulative loss.

Two other such programs were begun in vain in 1993. We hired a small Swiss manager to enter global interest rate swaps, mainly in Europe. That ended in early 1995 with a net loss of about $2 million. Our first use of portable alpha in 1993 ended with large losses by the time it was terminated 1½ years later. The manager did tactical asset allocation using index futures and invested the cash in a long/short common stock arbitrage that was intended to be market neutral. Both of these programs proved far more volatile than we had been led to believe.

Ironically, we made increasing use of portable alpha programs later in the 1990s, and with good success. But we paired a specialist manager of index futures with a market neutral arbitrage manager, although neither manager was aware of the other.

Another program we tried briefly, and unsuccessfully, in the 1990s was a market neutral long/short program in Japanese stocks.

Converting Cash to Equities

Selling the Losers wasn't our only challenge for Boston Safe. We believed (and I still do) that over the long term any cash is a meaningful drag on long-term performance. Each of our managers kept a certain amount of cash in our portfolio, on average perhaps 5% of the portfolio. To get rid of that, we started up KREF—the Kodak Reserve Fund.

We told each of our managers to keep in our account whatever amount of cash he felt comfortable with, but he could not manage it—even though he would continue to be paid for doing so. Every night Boston Safe would siphon off all cash to our KREF account. We instructed Boston Safe to credit each manager's deposit in KREF with whatever interest rate Boston Safe paid on its Short Term Investment Fund, and each manager could withdraw any amount of his cash any day he wanted. There was almost no chance, of course, that all managers would want to use all their cash at once.

KREF was, in effect, our own bank. The manager's deposits were KREF's liabilities. And we expected KREF to earn more on its investments than it paid the managers in interest. To achieve this, we invested most of the money in a series of common stock mutual funds (which would provide overnight liquidity if we ever needed the cash—and we didn't). We placed the rest of KREF assets with an aggressive specialist in cash management, who most often earned higher returns than the interest rate KREF had to pay on deposits. KREF was a highly profitable venture most years, and by the end of the century had added some $200 million to KRIP's bottom line.

The assets of KREF, which originally went into mutual funds, subsequently went into a global tactical asset allocation equity account and, by the turn of the century, all cash became overlaid with S&P 500 index futures.

Operation Sweep

We had been pleased with the one-time review of KRIP by Steve Rogers and John Casey in 1979, and when shortly thereafter John brought us an innovative idea we were glad to listen. John believed there were a lot of outstanding but less well-known investment managers around the country who were currently managing relatively small amounts of money, and some of them would make great additions to our team of managers. John was rounding up a number of pension funds who would pay his firm some $30,000 to finance "Operation Sweep," which would be John's sweeping around the country to dig out, meet with, and evaluate these less well-known managers. Sponsors would receive a thorough analysis of each manager.

The idea intrigued treasurer Don Snyder and me, but I wasn't sure how we could make adequate use of that stack of manager analyses. I wanted RCB (Rogers, Casey & Barksdale) to be accountable. So I said we would be a sponsor only if, at the conclusion of Operation Sweep, RCB would start up a commingled fund of the best of these managers in which we could be an investor. John agreed, and in 1981, began the RCB Trust composed of 10 or a dozen small managers, in which KRIP was the first investor.

We expected big things from the RCB Trust, but they never materialized. Why? In retrospect, I believe a key reason was that most of the managers selected had relatively short track records, typically five or six years, in a market that was highly skewed. Small stocks and value stocks, for example, had become so cheap by the mid-1970s that any investor focusing on them found the game to be like shooting fish in a barrel. There were no good benchmarks tailored specifically to small stocks (the Russell 2000 small-stock index came along only as of 1979) nor to value stocks. So all managers focusing on those sectors looked outstanding relative to the S&P 500. In 1989 KRIP was the last participant to give up on the RCB Trust.

Dividends from Operation Sweep

Operation Sweep was still a valuable venture for us. One of the first names John Casey came up with was a Fidelity manager named Peter Lynch, who since 1976 had managed Fidelity's Magellan Fund to returns that were double digits better than the S&P 500 every year! In 1982 Don Snyder and I visited Peter and were tremendously impressed. We asked Fidelity management if it would set up a commingled fund in its Fidelity Trust Company to be run by Peter. Peter and Fidelity agreed, and we immediately put $50 million (and subsequently more) into the new fund.

Hiring Peter Lynch was perhaps the best single manager selection we ever made, as somehow Peter continued his fantastic performance. Per our agreement at the outset, Fidelity soon closed Peter's commingled fund to new investors, while assets in his Magellan Fund soared as high as $50 billion. The Magellan Fund was so successful it became an American icon, but not surprisingly, Peter's commingled fund performed even better.

Peter soon had well over 1,000 stocks in the commingled fund, with turnover approaching 300% per year! How could anyone do that? Peter used Fidelity's research staff well. He'd gather his team around a table and give each analyst 60 seconds to describe his best find. And Peter worked with brokers directly, many of whom would give him their first call with a new idea, because they knew Peter would listen to anything, even though he was choosy as to what he would actually invest in. To me, this was an instructive lesson.

I recall an unforgettable vignette of Peter one time when he visited our Kodak office in Rochester for a meeting. He arrived early and asked to borrow my phone. He held the Wall Street Journal in one hand and tapped his foot as he reeled off a dozen or two buy and sell instructions to his trader. Peter was a genius, no doubt, but he was also the hardest working investment manager one could imagine. He was in the office for long hours seven days a week. In the fall of 1987 he went on his first vacation in years, taking his family to Ireland. Two days later the stock market went into an historic tailspin, and Peter was on his way home.

As a result, in 1989 Peter decided to retire at the tender age of about 46. He was managing by far our largest account, so we were devastated. From its rich talent pool, Fidelity chose Neal Miller to take over Peter's commingled fund. We redeemed a good portion of Peter's account, but based on our confidence in Fidelity management, we kept a meaningful amount in the account—another good decision. Neal proved to be our most productive manager through the 1990s.

At the same time we entered Peter Lynch's fund in 1982, we went into another new commingled fund at Fidelity, a high dividend-yielding U.S. common stock fund managed by Bruce Johnstone—whom John Casey had also identified through Operation Sweep. Bruce's track record wasn't as eye-popping as Peter Lynch's, but Bruce had outperformed the S&P 500 every year for the previous 10 years. Such consistency had to contain some solid predictive value. But shortly after the fund started up, Bruce began to underperform the S&P 500. And by the end of the 1990s, despite his continued dedicated work, Bruce had added no value to his benchmark. Bruce seemed to me as sure a bet as any manager we ever hired, and I never could figure out why he didn't come though. Eventually Fidelity moved Bruce to a different responsibility, and we pulled out of the fund.

When the RCB Trust expired in 1989 we hired directly two of its managers who had been very successful since its beginning in 1981.

One was Bill Sams, who ran the FPA (First Pacific Advisers) Paramount mutual fund. Bill was a one-man operation in a tiny office in Dallas who had a great network of brokers. He invested mostly in small, less-known stocks. The portfolio Bill managed for us was highly concentrated, perhaps fewer than 20 stocks, only his best picks. Bill's results were volatile but very little correlated with the rest of the stock market, and his compound results were outstanding, even though he generally kept a high level of cash (which, of course, we really invested in KREF).

We kept some $50 million with Bill (withdrawing assets as they increased above that amount), and Bill continued to do well for us in the 1990s. His mutual fund was kept small and closed to new investors. After a particularly successful year, however, Bill opened the mutual fund and quickly gained a sizable amount of new assets. Whether coincidence or not, Bill's subsequent performance deteriorated, and in time we parted company.

Bill was a good example of why managers should never meet with committees. Bill could never explain his investment approach cogently, and he always sounded like doomsday. No committee would have hired him. In his case, articulateness was inversely proportional to his investing ability. Bill never visited our office in Rochester, as he didn't like to fly.

From the defunct RCB Trust we also hired Warren Marcus of WRM Equity. Warren had been an outstanding bank analyst for Salomon Brothers before John Casey hired him in 1981 to manage a portfolio of small bank stocks. Warren and an assistant managed the portfolio from their small Westchester office. Probably no one throughout the country knew small banks as well as Warren, and we could afford to keep about $50 million in a tiny niche like that. At times we were Warren's only client. And was it worth it! Throughout the 1990s, Warren had the highest compound rate of return of any of our managers.

Results for 1979–82

As happened so many times over the years, our timing was poor when, in 1979, we chose to build up our index fund to more than $1 billion—a peak in 1980 of 56% of total Trust Fund assets. For the four years 1979–82, active managers generally surpassed the S&P 500—for the simple reason that active managers can invest outside of the 500 stocks in the index, and stocks outside of the index performed far better than the S&P 500 during that interval. The new Russell 2000 index of small stocks, for example, performed 10 percentage points per year better.

Over those four years, our benchmark—the S&P 500—compounded 16.1% per year. Our Trust Fund performed marginally better, thanks to our active managers. Because of our 100% equity orientation, we looked very good against other funds' total returns, but we were slightly below our target of other funds' results on equities only.

Our allocation to an index fund decreased little by little over time as we gained increasing confidence in our ability to select good active managers, and by 1993 the last of our index fund allocation disappeared. Our use of an index fund reappeared in 2000, but in the form of index futures overwritten by a portable alpha. That's another story we'll discuss later.

Staffing

Throughout most of the 1970s our performance and other data was assembled for me by a young professional in another part of the building. It seemed to me that such routine work was inappropriate for a professional, and about 1979 I arranged for the work to be done by a high-level clerical person. I also had a secretary who spent about half her time working on letters from shareholders (a responsibility I carried through the mid-1980s).

In 1982 things began to come together. I was named director, pension investments, and became a member of Kodak's "middle management." The clerical assistant had begun to devote full-time to pension investments and moved to an office adjacent to mine. And in June a top-flight associate was added to my staff. Duff Lewis, an engineer with the equivalent of an MBA from Purdue, had been with Kodak for 20 years and had distinguished himself on the corporate staff that analyzed potential investments for the Kodak company. Moreover, Duff had long been personally interested in investments. Duff proved an outstanding partner for the next nine years. He was the only member of our staff to earn a CFA (certified financial analyst) certification.

Besides KRIP, our staff continued to have responsibilities for the investment of Kodak's 401(k) plan ($2 billion, growing to more than $5 billion), and for assisting nearly 20 subsidiaries abroad with the investment of their pension plans (over $1 billion, growing to $2 billion).

Rogers, Casey & Barksdale continued to work with us as a consultant to KRIP. But John Casey and his staff rarely knew what managers we were hiring or terminating, as we never used RCB for its "Good Housekeeping seal of approval." We used it mainly as an extension of our own staff when there were projects we didn't have time to do or for which RCB seemed to have greater expertise than we.

Chapter 3

The Road to Diversification

Offsite Conferences for the Committee. In 1982 John Casey came to us and said, "You know what you ought to do? You should get your committee [KRIPCO] off site for a couple of days and simply blue sky ideas with a diverse group of leaders from the investment world." Because KRIPCO included the company's CEO and president, those particular individuals were not able to devote that kind of time. But the idea still seemed appealing, and we set it up in the fall of 1982 at Kodak's Marketing Education Center, across town from the main office in Rochester, N.Y. John Casey lined up a group of impressive investment icons to take part in our conference:

- Roy Neuberger,
- Dean LeBaron, founder of Batterymarch, whom we had hired in 1979 as a manager of U.S. common stocks,
- Francis Finlay, who had distinguished himself managing international stocks for Morgan Guaranty before starting up his own firm, Globe, Finlay,
- Alan Patricof, well-known sponsor of a number of venture capital funds, and
- Meyer Melnikoff of Goldman, Sachs, a retired Prudential executive who had been responsible for Prudential starting up its commingled real estate fund at the beginning of the 1970s.

The latter three never did manage any assets for KRIP.

Participating from Kodak were two KRIPCO members—CFO Bob Sherman and treasurer Don Snyder—plus future CFO Paul Smith, assistant treasurer Hal Passer, a legal staff member, and Duff Lewis and I. Steve Rogers and John Casey served as moderators.

I started the conference with a brief presentation about our current investment concepts and strategy, for the purpose of offering our guests a dart board. Steve and John then asked something like, "What's the first piece of advice you would give Kodak?" Each guest spoke in turn, answered inquiries from the Kodak group, and debated with one another. Over the two days Steve and John may have posed a dozen or more such questions. The results pried open the minds of our Kodak team.

"They don't all agree with one another!" observed one Kodak participant. But our guests all agreed that most pension funds invested much too narrowly in U.S. stocks. Inclusion of non-U.S. stocks, real estate, venture capital, oil & gas, and other asset classes would make a lot of sense. Subsequently, when we reviewed the conference with the full committee, KRIPCO decided to target 15% of our Trust Fund in private investments, mostly real estate, a target to be achieved within five years but to be done only on an opportunistic basis. In 1991 KRIPCO raised the target for illiquid investments to a range of 34 to 40% of KRIP assets by 1995. Private illiquid investments, however, peaked in 1994 at 29% of KRIP assets.

The conference also reinforced our drive to hold a sizable portion of our U.S. equities in small stocks, and to investigate the best way to get meaningful holdings in non-U.S. stocks. The overall benchmark for our Trust Fund was no longer the S&P 500, but the Wilshire 5000. Our belief was that our feet should be held to the fire of not just the largest U.S. stocks but *all* stocks traded in the U.S., including small stocks and foreign stocks that were listed here.

The idea of pursuing non-U.S. stocks was timely, but the increasing emphasis on small U.S. stocks, as good an idea as it was for the long term, could hardly have been timed worse. A curtain seemed to drop on July 1, 1983, and small stocks—which had been rising to the moon relative to large ones—reversed course, and the Russell 2000 underperformed the S&P 500 by 9 percentage points per year for the next six years.

It is hard to place a value on Rogers' and Casey's idea for the conference and their implementation of it. They personally helped us subsequently with six other such conferences over the next 17 years. Each subsequent conference was held at an attractive conference center—such as at Nantucket and Williamsburg. After each conference, we listened carefully to the "takeaways" and refined our asset allocation and strategy. If RCB never did another thing for KRIP other than those conferences, it would have more than earned its fees over the years.

When Harry Kavetas joined Kodak as CFO in 1994, we told him how valuable these conferences had been and asked if he would like us to plan another. Without much enthusiasm Harry said yes, and we arranged for a two-day conference in May 1995 at the Graylyn Conference Center in Winston-Salem, N.C. Guests included:[5]

- Roy Neuberger,
- John Templeton, another of the most successful and respected investors of the 20th century,
- Lew Sanders, the long-time wisdom behind the pension investing of prestigious Sanford Bernstein,
- David Fisher, CEO of Capital Research & Management, one of the oldest, most successful investment management firms, and
- Jeff Skelton, principal of a creative new investment firm in San Francisco, Symphony Asset Management.

Shortly before the conference, Harry Kavetas told me he was too busy and couldn't attend. We finally convinced him to come for part of the conference. Halfway through the conference, when Harry had to leave, he called everyone together and said something that I, or anyone I knew, could never have believed would come out of Harry's mouth. "I want you to know," he said, "that I have taken part in untold numbers

---

5.   Other KRIP conferences were held in 1987, 1991, 1993, 1997, and 1999. Guests at these conferences, besides Roy Neuberger and John Templeton, both of whom attended multiple conferences, included:

Peter Aldrich	Fred Grauer	Hilda Ochoa
John Angelo	Hank Hermann	Steve Roberts
Jack Bogle	John Hill	Barr Rosenberg
Gary Burkhead	Phil Horsley	Rex Sinquefield
Bill Crerend	Bill Jacque	Mark Tavel
Ray Dalio	Ron Kahn	Antoine vanAgtmael
Gilbert deBotton	Scott Lummer	Brian Wruble
Tim Ferguson	Peter Lynch	Buzz Zaino
Dale Frey	Ed Mathias	Dick Zecher
Jeremy Grantham	Sharmin Mossavar-Rahmani	

of conferences over the years. But this one is, by far, the most valuable I've ever attended. I can't tell you how sorry I am to be leaving."

Venture Capital

Somehow in 1982 we learned that the University of Rochester's endowment fund had some investments in oil & gas, so within a week or so of when Duff Lewis joined our staff in June 1982, he and I drove across town to meet with Phil Horsley, the university's head of endowment investments. Some relatively small oil & gas investments had been contributed to the university's fund in the 1950s, and it took little time for us to pick Phil's brain about them.

Phil then asked if we would like to see the rest of his portfolio, and we were astonished to find that a full 25% of the market value of the endowment fund was invested in venture capital partnerships. I asked Phil what internal rate of return the fund had earned from those partnerships over the last 10 years, and Phil replied that the return was very good but he didn't know what it was exactly. I asked if Duff could look at all the cash flows in and out of the university's venture capital investments over the last 10 years and calculate the internal rate of return (IRR), to which Phil readily agreed. The resulting IRR was an eye-popping 37%!

I had always thought venture capital would be a super asset class for a long-term oriented pension fund, but I never could conceive how we could get the expertise to know which venture capital firms to hook up with. Now, here was great expertise right in our own back yard!

"Phil," I said, "how would you like to manage venture capital partnerships for two funds—your university endowment fund and Kodak's pension fund?" Phil was so taken with the idea that he and his associate, Kevin Keogh, soon resigned from the University of Rochester and started up their own firm in Rochester—Horsley, Keogh and Associates—to invest in venture capital partnerships. The University of Rochester agreed to become their first client, and Phil and I hoped Kodak would be their second.

The matter was complicated by the risk-averse nature of Walter Fallon, Kodak's CEO. Finally, in February 1983, KRIPCO excluded Duff and me from its meeting, met with Phil Horsley (the committee's first and only meeting with a manager), then emerged to tell us it had approved our recommendation.

KRIPCO made a multi-year commitment for Horsley, Keogh to invest $100 million in a couple of dozen different venture capital partnerships, and to invest another $50 million side by side with those partnerships in individual start-up ventures that needed more money than the partnerships could finance. The latter strategy had worked well for Horsley at the University of Rochester, but it didn't for us.

Hindsight is always 20/20, but it soon became clear that we had jumped into venture capital right at the top of the market. The money going into venture capital had ramped up as the IPO (initial public offering) market became more and more exciting, and so had the pricing received by new ventures. In 1983 the IPO market seemed to shut down, and most venture capital partnerships that were started in 1983–84 made little if any money.

Horsley, Keogh (today, Horsley, Bridge Associates in San Francisco) in 1985 started up a series of venture capital fund-of-fund partnerships—seven of them through the year 2000—and Kodak committed sizable amounts of money to each. Our dollar-averaging approach took a long while to pay off, as the internal rate of return on all of Kodak's investments with Horsley, Keogh through 1993—10 years after the startup—was only 3%. What an opportunity cost, compared with the Wilshire 5000's return of 15% over those years!

But all of Horsley's fund-of-fund partnerships were eventually successful, increasingly so as time went by. And by the end of 1999, KRIP's internal rate of return on all its Horsley investments—weighted down by its inauspicious start in 1983–84—was a full 20%. One-year returns in the late 1990s reached as high as 300%. All of Horsley's funds proved to be in the upper part of the top quartile of venture capital funds that were started in the same year, and the firm of Horsley, Bridge remains arguably the premier manager in its field today.

The End of Buying Annuities

For many years I was convinced that annuities were a terribly expensive way to fund pensions, but Kodak continued to buy a Metropolitan annuity on every Kodak employee as he retired. My desire for change was stymied by KRIPCO. CEO Walter Fallon, referred to within Kodak as "the 800-pound gorilla," stated clearly at one KRIPCO meeting that he thought "annuities are the right and proper way to fund pensions."

As time went by, the evidence became more and more convincing, and our investment conference of 1982 helped to make this clear. During May 1993, shortly before the KRIPCO meeting where I made the recommendation to stop buying annuities, a KRIPCO member who was Kodak's general counsel, Ken Cole, met with Walter Fallon to remind him that under ERISA each KRIPCO member had a responsibility to act in his individual fiduciary capacity rather than as Walter's employee. As a result, the vote in favor was unanimous, except for one abstention—Walter's. That decision contributed more to the long-term investment return on KRIP than any other single decision.

But here we were with some $1.1 billion tied up in low-yielding annuities with Metropolitan. I expressed our frustration to our friends at Metropolitan, and they made a positive response. They allowed us to take several hundred million dollars out of the last couple of years' investment cells and put them in GICs (guaranteed investment contracts) at whatever rate Metropolitan was then selling GICs to clients. We jumped at the opportunity and locked up the money in GICs with an average duration of 6½ years at an average interest rate of 15.5%. That proved to be a lot more than Metropolitan annuity holders subsequently earned from their investment year cells, and it compared well with our common stock returns over that time.

As the GICs matured, Metropolitan allowed us to have the proceeds reinvested in any separate account (such as a common stock account) managed by Metropolitan. Since there were no Metropolitan separate accounts we would otherwise have chosen, we asked if Metropolitan could set up an S&P 500 index fund. Because index funds were not a specialty of Metropolitan's, our indexed money would not be as efficiently managed as at American National Bank of Chicago, but the difference would be relative pennies, so we terminated our Chicago account.

After Metropolitan purchased State Street Research and Management in Boston during the mid-1990s, Metropolitan allowed us to invest much of our annuity assets in any State Street account or, later, also in an REIT management firm, European Investors Inc., with whom Metropolitan had an affiliation. Through these steps we were by 1996 able to get the amount that was locked up in Metropolitan's annuity general account below 1% of KRIP's total pension assets.

Calculating Contributions

Until 1982 Metropolitan Life calculated the company's annual contributions that Kodak was to contribute each year to the pension fund. Initially Metropolitan used a unit credit actuarial method. Then in 1970 a switch was made to the Entry Age Normal method—a method used by most companies for many years thereafter. Under that method, the actuary calculated the uniform average percent of pay Kodak would theoretically have to contribute over the career of every employee and then applied that percentage to Kodak's total payroll. The result was contributions that reached a low of 6½% of payroll in the early 1970s and rose to a high of 12% in 1981.

I thought the Entry Age Normal method resulted in contributions that were higher than necessary, because if ever Kodak should freeze the plan—that is, terminate future benefit accruals—the pension plan would have far more money than it would need to fund its pension promises. I believed a plan sponsor should target a reasonable margin of assets above such termination requirements, but there was no reason why that margin should be huge.

I also felt that our actuarial assumptions were unrealistic and were another reason why our contributions were much larger than necessary. Initial key assumptions in 1970 were 5¼% return on assets and 4% annual increase in salaries. These assumptions were increased in 1974 to 6¼% return and 5% salary increase and remained unchanged through the early 1980s. In 1982 I proposed a change in our actuarial method to the less widely used Projected Unit Credit Method and to assumptions of 9% investment return and 6% salary increase. The acceptance of this recommendation led to an immediate end to the company's contributions to KRIP. By coincidence, a Projected Unit Credit Method was adopted in 1986 by the Financial Accounting Standards Board in its FAS 87 standard for pension accounting. Before long nearly all private pension funds were using some form of that actuarial method.

Kodak contributions went out with a bang in 1982. Because ERISA allows a range of permissible contribution levels, Kodak management chose to contribute close to the maximum—in the form of Kodak stock. CFO Bob Sherman gained approval for Eastman Kodak to contribute 3 million Kodak shares to KRIP in September 1982. The shares were valued by Goldman, Sachs at about $83 a share, or something over $240 million in all. Because KRIPCO believed it wasn't right for the pension fund to hold Kodak shares, we immediately took competitive bids from several investment bankers to underwrite the sale of those shares, and the winner was Morgan Stanley at about $94 a share. All the gain accrued to KRIP.

Two Contributions in 22 Years

That was Kodak's last contribution for many years. KRIP investment returns continued strong into the late 1980s, and its pension assets approached 80% more than the liabilities Kodak would need if it were to freeze the plan to future accruals.[6] CFO Paul Smith told Kodak's board of directors he expected Kodak would never have to make another contribution to KRIP in our lifetime. At that time, I felt that Paul had forgotten how another 1973–74 could come along at any time.

There was, in fact, concern at the time that a corporate raider might even try to buy Eastman Kodak Company and finance the acquisition partly by terminating the pension plan and using excess pension assets for the purpose. To do so, a raider would have to buy expensive annuities to cover all existing liabilities and then pay hefty taxes on remaining assets. I was one who didn't think that was a serious possibility. With close to 20% of our pension fund then tied up in private, illiquid assets, and more committed, the raider would have had a hard time coming up with the cash to buy expensive annuities and pay taxes, much less have usable cash left over.

In any case, the company eliminated that possibility in the early 1990s as it paid out huge sums to retirees in successive downsizing programs. In 1990 Kodak management changed the benefit structure to

---

6.   Specifically, the market value of assets was nearly 80% above ABO (Accumulated Benefit Obligations), as defined by the Financial Standard Accounting Board.

give each new retiree a choice between taking his pension in traditional monthly payments, or else receiving an equivalent lump sum. The government required that equivalent lump sums had to be calculated with an interest assumption that was driven by the interest rate on 30-year U. S. Treasury bonds, an extremely low interest rate that resulted in very high lump sums. In time, most Kodak retirees chose lump sums, receiving money that the pension fund could otherwise have invested for many more years at returns far higher than the 30-year bond rate. For 1991–99, KRIP payments to retirees averaged some 11½% of prior year pension assets—as much as $1.2 billion in a single year.

We raised cash to make these payments by writing our managers each quarter telling them how much money we would need from their accounts. To minimize transaction costs, we usually gave them up to 90 days to raise the cash. Kathleen Emert, who served as our administrative manager, proposed an amount to be raised from each manager based on which asset class was then overweighted relative to our target asset mix and which managers had grown larger than their normal allocations. Our staff discussed Kathleen's proposals but rarely made material changes. It was a relatively inexpensive way for us to continually rebalance our asset allocation toward our target allocation.

In the summer of 1991 Kodak temporarily sweetened retirement benefits in an effort to encourage 3,000 employees to retire. The company sweetened benefits so much, however, that closer to 8,000 employees retired, a further drain on pension assets.

By 1995 when Kodak brought in George Fisher as CEO and Harry Kavetas as CFO, one of their first actions was to stop allowing retirees to take lump sums on all benefits accrued after 1995. As a result of the hefty payouts to retirees, pension assets were only modestly above PBO liabilities,[7] motivating the new management to contribute $500 million in Kodak stock to the pension plan. Unlike 1982, however, Kodak management chose, contrary to the advice of staff, to retain the Kodak stock in KRIP, because management believed strongly that Kodak stock was materially undervalued by the market. KRIPCO hired the

---

7.   Projected Benefit Obligations, a going-concern calculation of pension
       liabilities, as defined by the Financial Standards Accounting Board.

Bank of New York as the fiduciary for the Kodak shares, including the responsibility to vote the shares. The shares were finally sold in 2003, and then at a price that was close to half the value at which they were contributed.

Kodak's only other contribution to the pension fund after 1982 was $170 million (in cash) in 1996. Those were the only two contributions Kodak made in 22 years. It would be interesting, though difficult, to calculate whether Kodak could have avoided any contributions at all since 1982 had it not been for the lump sum alternative provided to retirees in 1990 and the generous retirement incentive in 1991.

The Move from Core to Venture Real Estate

In 1983 KRIPCO added to the real estate commitments it had made in 1979. RCB recommended a partnership run by a dynamic real estate firm—JMB Realty in Chicago. After due diligence we recommended that KRIPCO commit to the fund about half of 1% of total Trust Fund assets. One of our committee members asked why, if we liked the program so much, we recommended such a small commitment to the fund. As a result, KRIPCO approved a commitment twice what we had recommended.

This was our last commitment to "core" real estate—properties purchased with the idea of holding them for 10 or 15 years or longer. We concluded that returns on core real estate simply were not attractive enough, despite the benefit of diversification. At the time, we didn't know how right we were. Returns on the RREEF and JMB funds turned out to be low single digits. Over the 15 to 20 years it took us to get the last dime of our returns from them, those investments represented a large opportunity cost to KRIP.

Instead of core real estate, we decided to target what we called "venture real estate." We wanted a real estate return *plus* an entrepreneurial return. We wanted managers who would buy properties to which they planned to add material value in a timely manner (as through construction, rehabilitation, or restructuring leases) and then sell the property to someone who wanted to buy some good core real estate. All properties should be sold within 3 to 7 years. The approach is far more management-intensive than core real estate and requires greater expertise, and more fees.

The concept also dealt with a major structural problem with core real estate programs such as RREEF and JMB. Annual fees for core funds equaled a percentage of the value of the properties, much as for a common stock manager. Managers had no incentive to sell properties opportunistically. In fact, they were highly motivated *not* to sell until required to do so by terms of the partnership agreement. When a common stock manager sells a holding he reinvests the proceeds in another asset and his fee remains the same. When a real estate manager sells a property, he usually must return the proceeds to investors. His assets go down, and his management fee goes down accordingly.

Negotiating Real Estate Fees

We quickly determined that all real estate fee structures should be based on an incentive fee, one that would make the manager's motivations as congruent as possible with our own. That means motivating the manager to sell when future expected net returns from a property fall below some hurdle rate.

If we wanted congruent motivations, then what was *our* motivation? A high rate of return—specifically a high *internal* rate of return, as time-weighted rates of return are inappropriate measures for a fund whose assets are built up and then sold. More specifically, we decided we would enter deals only if we could realistically expect a net IRR (net of all fees and costs) of at least 8% *real* (net of inflation, which was a particular worry at the time). We chose 8% real because that was at least 1% higher than we expected we could then earn from common stock investments.

At that time we found few if any real estate programs with such a fee structure. Typically incentive fees were calculated as a percentage of the value added to a property, regardless of how long the asset was held. We viewed such fees as totally inappropriate, because they failed to take into consideration the time value of money.

One of our early venture real estate proposals came in 1987 from the long-established organization of Cabot, Cabot & Forbes in Boston. Its proposed fee structure was inappropriate, however, and we said so. "Well," the manager had the temerity to respond, "what would *you* propose?" We were put to the test of figuring out what would be an appropriate incentive fee structure. We threw aside the KISS principle (keep it simple, stupid) and devised an incentive fee that could not be finally determined until the last property had been sold and the internal rate of return calculated. If the IRR was positive, the manager would receive a graduated percentage of all distributions to the investors until investors' IRR reached 8% real, after which the manager would receive 15% of all subsequent net profits.

Since the manager wouldn't receive any incentive fee until near the end of the program, he would need ongoing fees to keep him in business, so the fee structure also included an acquisition fee and an annual management fee based on the cost of the properties. The concept was that the fixed fees should provide no profit or high salaries for the manager. The manager's profit and high compensation should come entirely from the incentive fee. The concept, however, was much easier to articulate than to design.

Cabot's manager accepted our proposal, and then we asked our ERISA attorney, John Purves, to see if the fee structure would satisfy the requirements of ERISA. The Department of Labor (DOL) had indicated that a performance fee for a fiduciary may well be a *per se* prohibited transaction unless specifically exempted by DOL action. The problem could be avoided, however, if the investment met certain requirements whereby it would be categorized as *not* a Plan Asset under ERISA. John had to analyze the investment to make sure that it met those requirements and was appropriate from other fiduciary standpoints.

Negotiating partnership agreements was a continuing learning experience. One of multiple examples:

In 1986 KRIP entered a partnership with Public Storage to build ministorage warehouses, and Public Storage immediately took down some 25% of our commitment to the fund. Since Public Storage needed time to develop new properties, Public Storage held much of that money in cash equivalents for a long time. Never again! We required all future partnership agreements to allow the fund to draw money from its investors only on a just-in-time basis. We could earn much more from our cash than having it sit in a partnership's money market account. After we had entered two dozen private partnerships, KRIP would receive multiple demands for cash each week. We found we could readily fill these demands and still keep low-returning cash equivalents to a minimum.

As word got out that we might be interested in venture real estate opportunities, we had many visits by such managers. We did no deals that came through Wall Street, as they were too laden with fees. If a manager was in the early stages of recruiting clients for a fund, we were able to convince him to redesign his fee structure somewhat to our liking. Such managers were strong on real estate expertise but had only a short track record on fund management, as the fund they were marketing was only their first or second, and many properties in their prior fund had not yet been sold. A few managers had gained acclaim for their first couple of funds (even though their track records were short), and with those managers we had less bargaining power over fee structure and largely had to take it or leave it.

Results of Real Estate Investing

We had the misfortune of having some success with two of our first efforts in venture real estate. One was a hotel at Disney World, the other a beautiful office building on Pennsylvania Avenue in Washington. Our net IRRs on those were around 18%, but their duration was only about two or three years. And they turned out to be, in effect, an interest rate play instead of a real estate play. They were structured as convertible mortgages when interest rates were 15%. Also, Japanese investors helped us by buying the Washington building for some $300 million.

To restrain our enthusiasm about any given opportunity, we generally limited ourselves to recommending only half of 1% of Trust Fund assets to any one private, illiquid investment. By the end of the 1980s we were participating in some two dozen venture real estate partnerships. Some were tiny niche programs—such as a new shopping center in Maryland or a new office building in Pasadena—but when viewed together they were extremely well diversified by type (office, shopping center, warehouses, apartments, and hotels), by geography, and by size (some programs focusing on properties of $5 to $10 million, others on properties of $50 to $150 million). By the end of 1989 some 9% of KRIP assets was in real estate, with many commitments still outstanding.

As we built up our portfolio of venture real estate, the real estate accounts of Prudential, Equitable, and Aetna no longer fit into our strategy, and in 1989 we pulled out of those funds. It was one of the few occasions when our timing was fortuitous. Shortly after we pulled out, the commercial real estate market began to collapse and the United States entered its worst commercial real estate depression since the 1930s. Participants in those insurance company funds soon had to wait a year to get out, and then at much lower valuations.

We (and our real estate managers) had failed to recognize the increasing overbuilding that was going on throughout the 1980s. The overbuilding was driven partly by advantageous changes in tax laws and partly by the fact that bank loan executives were compensated by the *volume* of loans they placed, not *how profitable* they were. A given property might look exciting, but before the manager could add value to it and sell it, competing properties were being built, boosting vacancies to historically high levels.

None of the many venture real estate programs we entered in the 1980s, other than the first two, had attractive returns. Many returns were negative. Even some that we did in the early 1990s, when the pickings should have been good, were relatively mediocre. Our private real estate as a percent of total KRIP assets declined to 5% by the end of 1999. Over 20 years, the internal rate of return on all our real estate investments, burdened by the 1989–91 fiasco, was only about 6%.

About 1999 we were able to find managers of venture real estate who had longer, more reliable track records and from whom we expected net IRRs of 13% or more. Their programs looked increasingly attractive relative to the overpriced stock market. We began rebuilding our real estate commitments.

REITs

A few years earlier we added another real estate vehicle—real estate investment trusts (REITs). REITs are just another form of common stock, except that their income tax liability is passed on to shareholders (which is favorable for tax-exempt investors such as pension funds). REITs had been around since the early 1970s, but only starting about 1990 did the number of REITs devoted to *owning* properties begin to mushroom. There was no reason why general common stock managers couldn't invest in REITs, but few of them did. Investing well in REITs seemed to require special real estate expertise.

Although REITs trade like any other common stock and are influenced by stock market cycles, their volatility has had a relatively low correlation with that of the overall stock market, perhaps 0.4. That makes them an attractive diversifier.

REITs generally invest in core real estate. But some—despite the fact that they are allowed to derive no more than 30% of their gross income from the sale of property—are very aggressive and have strong venture components. At times when REITs are priced at a premium to the underlying real estate, the REITs can expand by buying more real estate and issuing more shares, or else by issuing more debt (within allowable limits). In this way, it is possible for REITs to achieve higher net returns over the long term than private core real estate funds. With this rationale, in the late 1990s we invested 1½% of KRIP assets with a manager who specialized in REITs.

Other Illiquid Investments
Shortly after Duff Lewis joined me in June 1982 we took a trip to Texas and Louisiana to look into opportunities in oil and gas, starting with a petroleum engineer in Fort Worth who had worked with the University of Rochester. We went down with the skepticism of a city slicker waiting to be fleeced. The small investment that resulted from that trip proved our skepticism was fully warranted.

In 1985 we hired Chase Investors (which later became part of UBS) to manage oil and gas investments and soon made commitments to two Morgan Guaranty commingled petroleum funds that subsequently resulted in low single-digit returns. Of course, the price of oil at the time we were making these initial commitments was some $25 a barrel, a price which by the mid-1990s had declined as low as $12.

It was obviously another example of poor timing. But we continued to believe in oil and gas as a solid high-return diversifier of our portfolio, and we kept dollar-averaging, investing with more entrepreneurial energy investors such as First Reserve. By the year 2000 these latter investments had pulled up our oil and gas internal rate of return since its inauspicious inception to about 10%.

In 1989 we entered a new asset class—timber. Increasingly, it became evident that the world's source of wood and wood pulp products would have to come from timber farms. We started with timber in the U.S. and during the 1990s moved into timber in such places as New Zealand and South America, where timber grows much faster than in the U.S. We did not expect flashy returns—just slightly above average returns that had virtually no correlation with the stock market. To a large extent, that's what we got, for an average internal rate of return since inception of about 11%.

Throughout the 1980s and 1990s we also participated in a couple of dozen leveraged buyout funds and other private corporate investment funds. This was another case of learning as we went, as the initial funds we entered in the 1980s were distinctly less than successful. But we kept at it, and by the end of the 1990s our internal rate of return since inception had exceeded 8%.

Another category we entered in 1992 was distressed securities. These programs were more successful and seemed increasingly timely as the quantity of distressed securities burgeoned after the turn of the century.

Kodak's First Market Neutral Investment

KRIP's first arbitrage program came in 1985, when we authorized KRIP's cash manager to invest in "synthetic cash." She could buy a market basket of stocks and sell S&P 500 index futures when the price of the futures got out of line. Subsequently, however, such arbitrage opportunities rarely occurred.

The year 1986 is when KRIP first began reaching out to truly alternative investments. Somehow, Duff and I heard of a different kind of manager, one whose volatility was low and had relatively little correlation with the stock market. That led us to visit Dick Nye of BDN in New York City. Dick had to explain his approach multiple times before we understood, but in essence, it turned out to be quite simple. When a merger was announced, Dick would do careful research—often including extensive legal counsel—as to whether the merger would actually be consummated. If it looked like a high probability, Dick would buy the stock of the company being acquired and, if the acquisition was for the acquirer's stock, sell short the acquirer. Thus, over the next few months, he earned the small difference between the acquiree's current stock price and the merger price. In the meantime, he didn't care whether the price of the two stocks went up or down. He was protected—unless the merger fell through, in which case he would lose his teeth (that is, lose *our* teeth). The key thing that grabbed our eye was Dick's track record over the past dozen years, where he had quite consistently earned net investment returns in the high teens.

There was, however, a problem. Besides his management fee, Dick wanted an incentive fee equal to 20% of all profits. Since BDN would be a fiduciary, any incentive fee would be considered a *per se* violation of ERISA, according to our attorney John Purves. John had Kodak's law firm submit a request to the Department of Labor for an Advisory Opinion blessing the fee structure. Surprisingly, the DOL responded fairly quickly with a favorable Advisory Opinion that contained a series of conditions the fee structure had to meet, all of which we could meet easily. It was the DOL's first Advisory Opinion blessing an incentive fee and one of very few ever issued by the DOL.

Accordingly, BDN (later named Baker, Nye) started up a merger-arbitrage account for KRIP in June 1986. The timing, as with so many of our actions, was less than the best. While BDN got off to a good start in its first year, the crash of the stock market in October 1987 led a number of announced mergers to fall through. Some merger arbitrageurs had big losses. Dick Nye, who always played it conservatively, also suffered losses, but they weren't great. He came back with some good years, including a 1989 return that was close to 30%!

The stock market turned negative in 1990, and the number of announced mergers dropped sharply. Dick had trouble finding enough to fill our portfolio, which had reached close to $100 million. He was astonished when, as a result, we removed more than $60 million from his account. But into the new century, Dick was still managing merger arbitrage for KRIP.

Eastman Kodak Company also hired Baker, Nye with its merger-arbitrage approach as the sole manager of the small Kodak Charitable Trust. That approach was an alternative to keeping all of the trust in a money market fund. Dick Nye earned returns that were quite consistently better than a money-market fund and with relatively low volatility. That demonstrated a reason why returns on merger-arbitrage are not higher: many Wall Street firms use merger-arbitrage from time to time as a substitute for money market investments.

Foreign Exchange

In 1984 KRIP made its first major move into non-U.S. investments, starting up a large global stock portfolio with the highly successful Templeton organization in Fort Lauderdale, Fla., which was still tightly supervised by the celebrated John Templeton himself. That exposed KRIP to the vicissitudes of foreign exchange fluctuations. Eastman Kodak Company's foreign exchange department under Eric Nelson had achieved great success in hedging the company's foreign exchange exposure, and in 1986 KRIP hired Eric's primary consultant, FX Concepts in New York, to hedge KRIP's exposure.

FX Concepts' fee structure was also to be built around an incentive fee. Our attorney, John Purves, spent a lot of time huddling with our tax attorney and outside ERISA counsel to see if the fee structure fit four-square with the conditions set in the DOL's Advisory Opinion on BDN. John finally gave his legal approval.

Soon it became apparent that we were leaving significant money on the table by limiting FX Concepts to simply hedging our foreign exchange exposure. FX Concepts could only sell a currency to hedge our exposure. It could never, for example, buy the British pound when it thought sterling was going to appreciate. And if FX Concepts believed the value of the yen was going to rise or fall but we had no exposure to Japanese stocks, it could not take advantage of that insight. So we unhinged FX Concepts from our actual exposure and told our manager he could go long or short on any currency as long as he didn't exceed certain net and gross exposure limits. We were treating foreign exchange as a *separate asset class*. We subsequently hired another of Eric Nelson's advisers to do the same thing.

Our currency managers earned modest net returns for us until about 1989, when Eric Nelson left Kodak and joined FX Concepts as a trader. Eric took over the KRIP account and has since done an excellent job with it.

Commodities

One day in 1987 I received a phonecall from a broker telling me about a tremendous commodity trader. I said we weren't interested in commodities. He asked if nonetheless he could bring the trader to visit us. True to our policy of never turning down an investment manager who wanted to see us, I reluctantly agreed. And hence we became acquainted with the commodity trading program of Mt. Lucas Management in Princeton, N.J.

Amazingly, the visit intrigued us enough that Duff and I flew to Princeton to visit Mt. Lucas, a learning experience. I had always thought commodity traders were dice rollers in a zero-sum game. The people at Mt. Lucas were Ph.D.s who were more like college professors. And they convinced us that trading commodities was, in a sense, like selling insurance. Most of the buyers and sellers of commodities were hedgers, protecting the price of their wheat crop or (since foreign exchange is one of the commodities) protecting the yen they were owed from Japan. Mt. Lucas had developed a very simple set of trading decision rules they called the MLM Index that took advantage of trending prices. Back tests over the prior 20 years showed that this "index" had, with significant volatility, earned meaningfully positive returns over that interval—returns that seemed entirely uncorrelated with stock market returns.

Mt. Lucas proposed to form a team of about eight independent commodity traders with complementary trading styles, and it set an incentive fee structure that was based on Mt. Lucas's results relative to the MLM index. The index would be calculated by an independent auditor and published in a trade journal. We proposed a trading limit and discussed this esoteric idea with attorney John Purves. John huddled with our tax counsel and outside ERISA counsel and even elicited a written opinion from the outside attorney. We knew of no pension fund that had ever done anything like commodities, but the favorable opinion was based on the facts of the matter and its likely advantages to the overall portfolio. KRIPCO approved the new program in October 1987.

We didn't give any money to either our foreign exchange or commodity traders to manage. Their programs were simply *overlays* of the rest of our portfolio. We placed a million dollars in the account of each at the beginning of a month to cover any losses they might incur, and we stood ready to add more money (rarely necessary) if losses were greater. At the end of the month, we peeled off any earnings they made that month and brought their account back to a million dollars for the start of the next month.

Mt. Lucas didn't hit a jackpot for us, but most years it earned a tidy additional return for KRIP.

Stock Lending

Starting in 1981, KRIP began earning, on average, $1 million or more per year by lending the stocks in its portfolio, in effect, to Wall Street market makers and short sellers. Because KRIP received cash collateral of more than 100% of the value of stocks being lent, and this collateral was marked to market every day, the income came with virtually no risk. KRIP was one of the early stock lenders, but as virtually all institutional funds began lending their securities, lending fees were driven way down.

In 1993 KRIP hired a dedicated lending agent, which proved advantageous for two reasons. First, KRIP's bias toward small and non-U.S. stocks made KRIP's stocks more attractive to borrowers than the typical institutional portfolio, resulting in slightly higher fees. The second had to do with investment of the cash collateral. Most of the T-bill rate of interest on the collateral has to be paid back to the borrower. Most lending agents (usually a fund's own custodian) handled investment of the collateral as part of a total stock lending package. KRIP, however, retained control of the investment of its cash collateral and placed it with its aggressive cash manager. Also, we estimated the portion of collateral that was more or less embedded, and we allowed our cash manager to invest that portion in longer maturities at higher interest rates. The result was that KRIP often earned more than $2 million a year in net stock-lending profits.

The Free Lunch

While analyzing the pattern of stock lending from the overall portfolio in 1983, Duff noticed that a large number of loans were made to a particular broker, but because the loans were for only two days, they didn't provide for much stock loan income for KRIP. The stock lending manager at KRIP's custodian, Boston Safe, explained that this was a common practice, allowing astute brokers to capture a premium on dividends paid by companies that provided shareowners the opportunity to reinvest the dividends in the common stock of that company at a discount—typically 5%. Wherever a company provided this discount, the broker would borrow the shares a day before the stock went ex-dividend, sign up for the dividend re-investment program, then immediately sell the new shares and return the borrowed stock the next day. The broker made a good profit for his effort.

Duff calculated that if we ourselves signed up for discount dividend reinvestment programs, there would be more than enough discount on reinvestment shares to cover a) all transaction costs to sell the shares, b) stock loan income that would be lost, and c) the fees charged by Boston Safe to execute these transactions. Once again, Boston Safe developed for us the systems necessary to make it all happen. The net result was additional income to KRIP of $80,000 to $100,000 per year well into the 1990s, until companies that provided the discount took away the free lunch. That profit wasn't much in the context of a multi-billion dollar portfolio, but still, it was a Free Lunch.

Directed Brokerage

In 1977 we had our first taste of directed brokerage. Standard brokerage commissions were well above a broker's cost for most transactions, and a third party lined up some brokers who offered to pay rebates directly to our Trust Fund when our managers executed trades through those brokers. We set up an arrangement like that, but legal concerns were raised, and we discontinued the program. Some years later, when our ERISA attorney, John Purves, and I visited about the matter with the Department of Labor's Office of Pension Administration in Washington, senior policy maker Mort Klevan told us he considered brokerage rebates inappropriate. Investment managers had a fiduciary duty to obtain the best total transaction costs (market impact plus brokerage expense), and if appropriate, the managers should simply use less expensive brokers.

Accordingly, we compiled a list of brokers who would execute trades—U.S. or non-U.S.—for 2 cents a share whenever the Kodak pension fund was involved in any portion of the transaction, and we urged our managers to use those brokers whenever they believed their use would lower total transaction costs. We did not direct our managers to use those brokers because we did not want to take away our managers' fiduciary responsibility to obtain the lowest total transaction costs. Some of our managers used these discount brokers, but some declined even though they might agree to use brokers who charged standard brokerage commissions but who would pay rebates to KRIP assets. In 1985, the first year of this program, with only a single 2-cent broker, we estimated a net savings of some $650,000 for the year.

Most other pension funds were using the rebate form of directed brokerage, and eventually it became clear that we were leaving some money on the table. Finally, in the late 1990s, we encouraged our managers to use *either* 2-cent brokers or rebate brokers. By 1999, broker rebates to KRIP assets amounted to nearly $250,000 per year.

Focus on Active Common Stock Managers

Despite all these alternative investments, Duff and I kept our eye on where most of our money was invested—in common stocks. We monitored our existing managers with our well-disciplined monitoring approach and kept looking for new managers who were even better. In the latter 1980s and through the 1990s we met with an average of nearly 100 managers a year *in addition to* those who already managed for KRIP. Whenever a manager visited us, all of our available senior staff (mostly, that meant all two of us) met with the manager. That was a key part of our R&D.

An exception occurred in 1979, shortly after restructuring KRIP's portfolio. Following a suggestion from Steve Rogers and John Casey, we hired Dean LeBaron's Batterymarch Asset Management to actively manage U.S. stocks. We were impressed by Dean's innovative computerized system, whereby he had detailed data about every stock in his computer. He could enter a series of criteria—such as P/E ratio no greater than X, earnings growth rate in excess of Y, and stock price volatility no greater than Z—and immediately get a printout of all stocks that met those criteria. This seemed to give Batterymarch a technological advantage over other managers. And indeed, for the first couple of years, Batterymarch put attractive returns on the board.

By the mid-1980s, however, Batterymarch's performance was lagging. Technological advantages don't last long in the investment world, and by then, most managers had a similar kind of computerized data bank. Dean LeBaron, of course, had become a special, much-appreciated friend of ours through his participation in our KRIPCO conference in 1982. Nonetheless, in 1985 Duff and I recommended termination, and KRIPCO agreed. We continued, however, to regard Dean LeBaron as a good friend.

Another Manager of Small Stocks

In 1983 the marketing representative of Lehman Brothers brought us the story of their outstanding manager of small stocks. Duff and I went to New York to meet him and were much impressed with Boniface "Buzz" Zaino, who had been managing extremely small stocks with an eclectic value bias since the mid-1970s. We prepared a recommendation to KRIPCO to place a sizable account with Lehman Brothers.

Two weeks before the KRIPCO meeting, news came that Buzz Zaino had left Lehman and joined Trust Company of the West (TCW) to manage stocks in the same way out of an office in New York. Duff and I took the recommendation we had prepared, crossed out the name of Lehman, and inserted the name of TCW. The poor Lehman representative who had worked so effectively to sell us the prowess of Buzz Zaino never received a nickel for his successful effort!

Buzz and his associates, Nick Galluccio and Susan Schottenfeld, did a superb job from the starting bell. For the next 17 years and more, TCW's account gave us net returns that exceeded the Russell 2000 by more than 4 percentage points per year! Buzz left TCW in the mid-1990s to manage money elsewhere, but Nick and Susan and their staff carried on without missing a beat.

A Chance to Make Amends

In the years ahead, we had opportunities to prove we had learned something from our 1974 fiasco when we terminated KRIP's participation in the Windsor Fund.

In 1984 we hired Sanford Bernstein & Company, a brokerage house that provided some of the best investment research on the Street and had begun in 1973 to manage pension money very successfully. Bernstein managed U.S. stocks with a deep value bias and for a few years performed extremely well. But its performance fell out of bed in 1989–90, and it lost a lot of its clients. Its investment architect, Lew Sanders, was extremely articulate about why its big bets—the banks and automobile companies—were tremendously undervalued. We stayed with Bernstein and reaped stunning rewards in the next few years.

The growth stock craze in the late 1990s brought on a similar bad period for Bernstein, which it more than made up for in the first year or two of the new century.

Quantitative Investing

In 1987 Duff and I became aware of another manager who seemed like a great opportunity for us—Barr Rosenberg in California. Barr had done acclaimed work as a Ph.D. in the 1970s by developing his "BARRA" factors to describe the distinctive characteristics of each stock that account for its stock price. He then started up a prestigious consulting firm called BARRA.

But in 1984 he left his consulting firm and started up a money management firm—now AXA Rosenberg Institutional Equity Management—to manage U.S. stocks by selecting a diversified portfolio of stocks that were most underpriced by the market. He put the prices of 5,000-plus U.S. stocks in a computer and derived, through a massive regression equation, the weights that the regression equation placed on each BARRA factor at that time. Barr's credibility was further enhanced by the fact that he had developed what was the most complete, up-to-date database we were aware of on every stock. Rosenberg started off very well for KRIP, but about 1990 ran into a performance problem that sent Barr Rosenberg back to his "drawing board" computer. Although not greatly intended, his approach had a bit of a value bias, which was damaging in a growth-stock era. Barr modified his algorithm, and Rosenberg's performance got back on track.

Over time, it became apparent to us that Rosenberg added materially more value to small stocks than large stocks. This came as no surprise, because we had long felt that large stocks were so well-researched and therefore so efficiently priced that even a great manager found it difficult to add a lot of value over an index fund. On the other hand, small stocks were less researched and therefore priced inefficiently enough that a good manager could viably outperform the Russell 2000 small-stock index by 3 to 4 percentage points per year. (That means, of course, that average investors in small stocks had to perform well below the index!) That small stock syndrome of value-added investing saved us to some extent in the 1980s, when small stocks so greatly underperformed large stocks.

Anyhow, in 1998 KRIP changed Rosenberg's account so the firm was managing for us a long/short account, mainly in small stocks.

Proxy Voting

During the 1980s much industry discussion focused on who should vote the proxies for a pension fund's common stocks, and how. KRIP had always had its investment managers vote proxies on the belief that each manager should know best what proxy votes would do most to enhance the value of its common stock holdings.

In 1990 I reported to KRIPCO on a study of the voting of KRIP's common stock managers, noting that in some cases where two managers held the same stock they voted the proxies differently. After some discussion, the committee concluded that proxy voting by our managers continued to be far superior to KRIPCO deciding any votes, and that differing votes on the same stock were entirely appropriate, because difference of opinions is what makes markets. KRIPCO also agreed that in our annual questionnaire to investment managers we should continue to elicit answers to the following two questions:

- Did you vote all proxies for stocks in our portfolio last year?
- Did you vote all of them solely in the interests of our plan participants?

Trust Fund Returns During the 1980s

As one might surmise, illiquid investments—as well as our bias toward small stocks and value stocks—proved, in retrospect, to have been an anchor around our neck in the 1980s. Even so, for the 10 years 1980–89 KRIP earned 16% per year, which ranked in the top 3% in U.S. pension fund performance, even though KRIP's total return didn't quite equal the median common stock return of other U.S. pension funds.[8]

As a result of the KRIPCO investment conferences in 1982 and 1987, the members of our committee understood what we staff members were doing and why. An illustration occurred in October, 1987, when the U.S. stock market plummeted some 25% in a week. The value of KRIP assets suddenly dropped by $1 billion. We happened to have a KRIPCO meeting scheduled at the end of October, and Duff prepared a one-page report on our losses. It took him little more than a minute to give the report, after which Paul Smith, who had succeeded Bob Sherman as CFO in 1984, looked around the table and asked, "Any questions?" Hearing none, he said, "Then let's get on with our next business." We had told KRIPCO for years that such a market debacle could happen at any time (as it always can), and it was satisfying to see that no one flinched when it did happen. On that particular occasion, the market bounced back strongly in the next six months.

One reason KRIP didn't get hurt worse by the October 1987 market debacle was a report to KRIPCO by Duff Lewis in December 1986 on "portfolio insurance." The concept, which had become popular at the time, was a way to limit losses that wasn't really *insurance*. Typically, portfolio insurance would have a fund hedge, say, 25% of its stock portfolio by selling S&P 500 index futures. When stock prices rose, the formula called for the repurchase of some of these futures. When stock prices fell, it called for the sale of more futures. Duff concluded with a strong recommendation that KRIP avoid portfolio insurance, because it was more expensive and risky than it was worth. Sure enough, when the October 1987 market crash occurred, and portfolio insurers tried to sell more index futures as the market plummeted, the

---

8.   Per the new TUCS (Trust Universe Comparison Service) universe of some 200 master trusts. At that time TUCS held the largest database of pension fund performance figures.

sudden illiquidity of the market made such transactions prohibitively expensive. In short, portfolio insurance didn't work and may have seriously exacerbated the market decline.

Our staff continued to consist of Duff and me and two clerical persons. One reason we could operate well with a small staff is that we spent most of our time looking after our investments and searching for new opportunities. We spent little time preparing reports. We gave KRIPCO a thorough report once a year, but only a one-page update at the end of each quarter. On one occasion, even that one-page report elicited criticism from KRIPCO chairman Paul Smith. "Rusty," he said, "you spend all this time trying to teach the committee members the importance of being long-term oriented, then you give them a golden opportunity to be myopic by circulating your quarterly performance report!" We discontinued the report, of course.

Another advantage was some independence from corporate budgets. Starting in 1986 Kodak was reimbursed from plan assets for travel and out-of-pocket administrative expenses for KRIP. And in 1989 such reimbursement also included a proportionate share of staff salaries and benefits, based on the respective staff persons maintaining a daily log of hours spent on KRIP as a percent of their total hours worked.

A further word about KRIPCO meetings. Aside from the detailed performance review that the staff gave the committee once each year, KRIPCO meetings were held only when staff had recommendations. All investment commitments, of course, had to be approved by KRIPCO. Typically, eight or nine meetings were held each year. The flexibility that was built into the scheduling of these meetings is illustrated by a comment Paul Smith made to me in the mid-1980s: "Rusty," he said, "I don't want to miss any good investment opportunities because of the inability to schedule a KRIPCO meeting. We'll find a way to have a KRIPCO meeting if necessary." Such special meetings were rarely necessary, but the remark roundly demonstrated the committee's support for KRIPCO's investment strategy and the work the staff was doing.

Although in the 1990s KRIPCO adopted different benchmarks in place of the Wilshire 5000 (the benchmark the committee had established in 1983), it is ironic to note that for the 22 years, 1983–2004, the annual rate of return on KRIP's total Trust Fund equaled 13.0%, a hair better than the Wilshire 5000, with much less volatility.

Chapter 4

The Roaring Nineties

KRIP got off to a poor start in the nineties. Hardly anything went right in 1990. Not only were private investments a drag, but small stocks, value stocks, and non-U.S. stocks—which KRIP had carefully overweighted compared with other pension funds—dramatically underperformed large U.S. growth stocks. KRIP's return of minus 4.7% was rock bottom among its peers for that one year. That pulled KRIP's five-year performance down to 10.5%, but still a hair above the median of other pension funds, according to TUCS figures. Fortunately, KRIP came back with exceptionally strong results in 1991.

After that, huge payouts to retirees loomed ahead—more than twice KRIP's highest prior annual payouts—a result of Kodak allowing retirees to take their pensions as a lump sum and Kodak's very successful early retirement incentives of 1991. To hedge against these costly lump sums and other large pension payouts, KRIP hired a manager to short S&P 500 futures. The short futures were intended solely as insurance, and in the end, KRIP paid a high premium for the insurance, as the market continued to charge ahead.

Non-U.S. Stocks

KRIPCO had made a serious entry into non-U.S. stocks in 1984 when it started up a global stock account with Templeton. We chose a *global* account instead of a *non-U.S.* account because we believed a good manager should be able to perform better if he had twice as many stocks to choose from. We subsequently changed our mind and made Templeton a *non-U.S.* account, as we concluded that no manager was brilliant enough as a market timer to know when to overweight U.S. or non-U.S. stocks.

KRIP soon added a commingled non-U.S. stock fund managed by Ed Barksdale of Rogers, Casey & Barksdale. For a change KRIP's timing was good. For the four years 1985–88 the index of non-U.S.

stocks[9] outdistanced the S&P 500 by 26 percentage points per year! Much of that was due to the exploding prices of Japanese stocks, which accounted for as much as 60% of the index (vs. closer to 20 to 25% today). KRIP didn't get full benefit because Templeton, which had previously made a ton of money investing in Japanese stocks, had in 1984 pulled completely out of Japanese stocks because Templeton thought they had gotten way overpriced. But KRIP's performance in non-U.S. stocks during those years was still very good compared with its U.S. investments.

The bonanza in Japanese stocks ended in 1988, however, and for the next 13 years non-U.S. stocks *under*performed U.S. stocks by some 11 percentage points per year. Nevertheless, all through the 1990s KRIP continued to build up its non-U.S. stock portfolio.

KRIP entered another new world in 1989 when we hired Antoine vanAgtmael's Emerging Markets Management in Washington, D.C. Antoine had in 1986 become one of the first institutional investors to invest in stocks of Third World countries. We hired his firm not only because of Antoine's expertise in those countries but because many Third World countries were growing much faster than the developed world, and their stocks carried significantly more attractive price/earnings valuations. Emerging markets stocks are volatile, and so has been the performance of Antoine's firm, but over the years it has done some 2 percentage points a year better than the index.[10]

In 1990 we hired a quantitative manager of *non-U.S. small* stocks—Acadian Asset Management in Boston—and we set a unique and extremely tough benchmark: the *equal-weighted* performance of the more than 3,000 stocks in Acadian's database, which because of equal weighting was essentially a small-stock index. For standard non-U.S. stocks in the mid-90s we added Grantham, Mayo & van Otterloo and Oechsle in Boston, and Morgan Stanley's London-based program. Then in 1998 we added another manager of small non-U.S. stocks, also managed out of Morgan Stanley's London office, and a second manager

---

9.   The Morgan Stanley Capital International (MSCI) index of stocks in Europe, Australia, and the Far East (EAFE), which was the most widely used index of non-U.S. stocks.

10.   The MSCI Emerging Markets Free stock index.

of emerging markets stocks, Capital International, which in 1986 also had been one of the pioneers in emerging markets stocks.

Overall, KRIP's managers of non-U.S. stocks achieved good *relative* performance during the 1990s. But because the non-U.S. index underperformed the S&P 500 by 11 percentage points per year during that decade, our non-U.S. stocks were a drag on our total fund results. Even so, KRIP continued to build up its non-U.S. portfolio until by the turn of the century non-U.S. stocks accounted for a full 40% of KRIP's total common stock portfolio.

Initial Use of the Efficient Frontier in Asset Allocation

Starting in 1991, we used Efficient Frontier analysis provided by Rogers, Casey & Barksdale to improve our asset allocation. An Efficient Frontier program is a computer program that calculates asset allocations that will provide the highest possible expected return at every given level of market value volatility. The results are totally dependent, of course, on the assumptions that are put into the model. For each asset class, one must input an expected rate of return, an expected volatility, and expected correlations with every other individual asset class. Clearly, any single set of assumptions will be wrong, because no one can foresee the future. The object, then, is to find an asset allocation that will hold up well under a wide range of different assumptions.

At our two-day KRIPCO conference in 1991, we showed our distinguished guests the results of an Efficient Frontier run and the assumptions that went into the run, and we asked each of our guests if he would like to submit alternative assumptions the next day, so RCB could calculate the results by noon. We were disappointed no one submitted alternative assumptions. We had to develop our own.

We almost always used the same expected return assumption for non-U.S. stocks as for U.S. stocks, because we couldn't see why either should give stronger returns than the other over the long term. Because non-U.S. stocks are more volatile but are less than fully correlated with that of U.S. stocks, the Efficient Frontier always told us we weren't including enough non-U.S. stocks. That was the reason for the continuing buildup in our non-U.S. stock allocation.

In 1989 a BARRA study of KRIP's portfolio of 22 common stock managers showed that the portfolio tended toward volatile, cyclical companies and had above-average turnover. It also showed that, with one exception, KRIP's 22 managers were complementary to one another. Our portfolio also continuously had an extreme small-stock bias. A typical comparison with the Russell 3000 index of U.S. stocks was:

Market Cap[11]	KRIP	Russell 3000
$0–300 million	17%	4%
$300–500 million	8	3
$500 million–$1 billion	12	6
$1–5 billion	24	23
>$5 billion	<u>39</u>	<u>64</u>
	100%	100%

KRIP's overall asset allocation also differed greatly from that of other large corporate pension funds. In 1995, for example, the comparison was as follows:

Asset Class	KRIP[12]	Average of Other Large Pension Funds[13]
U.S. stocks	34%	48%
Non-U.S. stocks	20	16
Fixed income	8	25
GICs and annuities	2	1
Cash	2	3
Market neutral programs	5	0
Real estate equity	13	4
Other	<u>16</u>	<u>3</u>
	100%	100%

11.   Market capitalization is the price of a stock times the number of shares that is outstanding (or the number that is freely tradable).
12.   Hard assets only, excluding overlay programs.
13.   Per Greenwich Research Associates.

25-Year Zeros

In 1989 Duff and I began to examine how we would expect our portfolio to react under different economic scenarios. The scenario in which our portfolio would perform worst was that of deflation—not a likely scenario then, but still possible. The best asset class to protect against deflation was a bond portfolio, but we didn't like the low returns we expected from bonds. How could we protect the portfolio with the smallest allocation to bonds? The answer: 30-year zero-coupon bonds that the U.S. Treasury had begun to issue.

We went to our only fixed income manager—who aggressively managed our cash—and asked her if she would like to manage a portfolio benchmarked against 25-year zero-coupon bonds (or "Zeros," as we called them). She said she could easily do that, and did, with a small portion of our portfolio.

In 1991 when Ray Dalio of Bridgewater Associates—a manager of fixed income derivatives—made a sales call on us, we mentioned our Zero program to him. Ray convinced us he could exceed the return on 25-year zero-coupon bonds with very little more volatility by buying interest-rate futures. Five interest-rate futures, each with a duration of about five years, would be about the same as a 25-year zero-coupon bond, and futures would be far more liquid. The futures would, in effect, leverage the five-year yield curve. Because the interest-rate on a 5-year bond is typically higher than on a 4½-year bond, the future would earn not only the bond yield but also a small capital gain on each future over the six-month holding period.[14] In addition, Ray assured us he could add value by going long or short interest rate futures of other countries.

The idea sounded logical, and because Ray had established an impressive track record, we moved our Zero account to Bridgewater, and over time Bridgewater added material value. We subsequently had Bridgewater manage two other small accounts, both as overlays to our overall portfolio, with no hard assets, just like our commodities program. We structured them as overlays because we expected both programs to have a zero or slightly negative correlation with our

---

14.   Assuming no change in the "yield curve" of interest rates.

overall Trust Fund. In 1993 Bridgewater invested the first account in its "global macro" program, with a portfolio of some 50 diverse futures. In 1994 Bridgewater invested the second account in low-volatility inflation-linked bonds in the U.K., Canada, and Australia. Bridgewater managed the second account entirely with swaps. Its swap counterparty invested in a portfolio of inflation-linked bonds as directed by Bridgewater, then Bridgewater swapped the return on U.S. Treasury bills plus a fraction of a percent for the return on the counterparty's inflation-linked portfolio.

More Fixed Income

Ray Dalio also showed us analyses demonstrating that virtually all familiar asset classes, if leveraged up or down to the same volatility level, had historically achieved roughly the same long-term rate of return. As we saw it, that meant if a manager leveraged up a bond portfolio to the stock market's long-term volatility, the manager should be able to achieve about the same return.

In 1994 Bob Spooner and I obtained from Rogers, Casey & Barksdale the names of four top-flight bond managers and asked each, "How would you like to run a bond portfolio with no constraints except you are not to incur volatility greater than that of the S&P 500?"

Each responded enthusiastically much the same way: "No one has ever asked us to do that, but that's really the way to manage fixed income. We could do a great job for you." So we put a modest amount of money with the each of the four bond managers. One manager bit the dust in a couple of months, leveraging up emerging markets debt well beyond S&P 500 volatility. We dropped another manager after a couple of years because he couldn't seem to add value. The other two seemed like good additions to our portfolio. One was eclectic, while the other invested exclusively in emerging markets debt and high yield bonds. That manager didn't seem to add value by his timing between the two, so we divided the manager's account in two—one account devoted entirely to emerging markets debt, the other to high yield bonds.

As the 1990s progressed we added six more bond accounts—one in inflation-linked bonds, two more in high-yield bonds, one more in emerging markets debt, and two global bond accounts. For our historically equity-oriented Trust Fund, we had made a material foray into fixed income.

More Market Neutral

During the first few years of the 1990s we increased our allocation to market neutral investments. We added a second merger arbitrage manager, and in 1991 we discovered a creative fixed income arbitrageur in a college professor named Doug Breeden in Chapel Hill, N.C.

Doug's firm, Smith Breeden, specialized entirely in mortgage investments. Doug showed us how his firm could earn good returns by buying (or selling short) mortgage investments such as FNMAs and GNMAs and arbitraging them against U.S. Treasury bills through the use of interest rate futures, earning money on the changing spread between mortgage and T-bill interest rates. The unleveraged return was puny, but we authorized Smith Breeden to leverage its arbitrage two to 10 times, which sounds wild. It wasn't. It appeared as if, even with this much leverage, the program would be significantly less volatile than the S&P 500. Most intriguing to us, the returns were expected to have a modest *negative* correlation with returns on the stock market. As expected, Smith Breeden didn't shoot the lights out, but over the long term it did earn low double-digit returns with relatively low volatility and a modest *negative* correlation.

In 1993 we hired a manager dedicated to convertible arbitrage—buying convertible securities and selling short the common stocks into which those securities were convertible. During the 1990s we hired seven other market-neutral managers. We hired additional ones in merger and acquisition arbitrage and in distressed securities, and four common stock arbitrage managers—ones who sold short a portfolio of common stocks equal in value to their long portfolio of common stocks.

Portable Alpha

In 1998 we began incorporating some of our market neutral programs into a *portable alpha* approach. We had an international tactical asset allocation (TAA) account that was invested entirely through the use of stock index futures. All the hard assets in the account were initially in cash equivalents, as T-bill returns are assumed in the pricing of futures. Instead of leaving the hard assets in cash, we invested them in one of our market neutral accounts. Any return earned by that account in excess of T-bill interest rates would be considered an alpha, which we "transported" to the tactical asset allocation account by adding it to the return on that account.

Then at the beginning of 2000 we instituted what we called our *master portable alpha* program. Instead of attaching a particular market neutral account to a particular futures account, we funded initially 13 market neutral programs from a "portable alpha trust." That "trust," in turn, was funded by the cash from separately managed programs that invested in S&P 500 futures, interest rate futures (our Zero accounts), and TAA index futures. The average return on those market neutral programs in excess of T-bill returns was then added to each of the futures programs—resulting in handsome "transported alphas." By early 2000 we allocated some 22% of KRIP's portfolio to this master portfolio alpha program.

A Directional Hedge Fund

Market neutral funds are often referred to as hedge funds, but I have tended to think of them as distinct from hedge funds. Hedge funds, by my definition, are both long and short stocks (or other) securities, but they are almost always net long, and therefore not market neutral. We were skeptical of directional hedge funds because they typically charge a 1% management fee, much higher than most common stock funds, *plus* 20% of all profits. It is hard enough for a normal common stock manager, net of fees, to outperform an index fund. A hedge fund would have to be phenomenal to overcome the heavy drag caused by such fees.

In 1991 we did, however, add a single hedge fund to our portfolio— the Jaguar Fund. Its founder and chief investment officer, Julian Robertson, had established Tiger Management and the Jaguar Fund about 1980 and had consistently put spectacular returns on the board. Jaguar rewarded us with some great years, which led Tiger to become KRIP's largest single manager. In line with our policy of rebalancing to our target portfolio, we redeemed each year a portion from the Jaguar

Fund. But we weren't the only one to admire what Julian Robertson and his organization were doing. As a result, assets of the Jaguar Fund zoomed well past $10 billion. That should have been our signal to quit while we were ahead, because it is unreasonable to expect a fund that size to perform nearly as well as it did when it was one-third the size. Sure enough, the Jaguar Fund ran into a period of poor performance about 1998, and many investors pulled out at the same time. The sale of Jaguar's most liquid assets left the fund with assets which, in an illiquid market, continued to decline. We exited too, but far later than we should have.

A Summary of Alternative Investing

Following is a summary of how KRIP entered investment areas that may at the time have been considered "alternative investments." The more areas we entered, the more confidence we gained about entering further new areas. And even though not all new areas were success-ful, we became increasingly confident in the overall strength that this diversification added to KRIP's portfolio. We didn't try to enter these areas all at once, but we learned more and more over time.

1977	Index funds	1989	25-year Zeros
	Directed brokerage commissions		Emerging markets stocks
1979	Core real estate		Timberland
1981	Selling short		Interest rate futures
	Stock lending	1991	Hedge funds
1982	Equitized cash		Mortgage arbitrage
1983	Venture capital	1992	Distressed securities
	Discounted dividend reinvest		Long/short stocks
	Selling call options		Private European firms
1984	Global stocks	1993	Portable alpha
	Oil & gas properties		Convertible arbitrage
	Trading S&P 500 index futures		Global tactical
1985	Venture real estate		asset allocation
	Discount brokers		Interest rate swaps
	Synthetic cash	1994	High-yield bonds
1986	Leveraged buyouts		Emerging markets debt
	U.S. tactical asset allocation		Inflation-linked bonds
	M&A arbitrage		Private Asian companies
	Foreign exchange trading	2000	Master portable alpha
	Commodity futures		program

A Change in Regime

In 1991 Kodak offered phenomenal financial incentives to encourage veteran employees to retire. It hit home when my outstanding partner, Duff Lewis, then 52 years old, came to me and said, "I don't see how I can retain my reputation as an astute investor if I turn down this retirement package." A factor may also have been that, despite the high esteem in which the members of KRIPCO held Duff, and despite the fact that there were years when the pension fund earned more than the Kodak company itself, Kodak management didn't want to allot two "middle management" positions to the function of pension investments. So Duff felt there was a roof over his head.[15]

After we had worked together so closely for nine years, losing Duff was a big blow to me, because I didn't know how I could obtain an equally competent partner. My concern was for naught. Within a month I was able to select a 20-year Kodak veteran who was an engineer with a Ph.D. in finance from the prestigious Wharton School— Bob Spooner. Bob was a full partner and major contributor in all that we did in the coming decade. And, ironically, he was already a member of Kodak's "middle management."

After nine years as CFO and chairman of KRIPCO, Paul Smith retired in 1993. The record of Paul's last KRIPCO meeting includes the following sincere words of tribute I made:

> You and the outstanding individuals who have composed KRIPCO have brought demanding and questioning minds to the table—but always open minds, free from second guessing.... In my discussions in the field, I have often held up you and the members of KRIPCO as a model of how a pension committee ought to work.... And beyond all of your sagacity and fiduciary prudence, you are a fun group with whom to work.

---

15.   Duff joined Rogers, Casey & Associates in late 1991 as a managing director, then in 1996 returned to Rochester as an investment officer with the University of Rochester. He retired from the university in 2004.

In December 1993 Kodak gained a new CEO, George Fisher, and within a month he brought in from IBM a new CFO, Harry Kavetas. I met Harry for the first time at a social function in January 1994, when Harry smiled at me and said softly, "Rusty, I'm going to be the death of you."

I soon discovered what he meant. Harry believed the right way to invest pension money was through index funds, whereas we had just redeemed the last of ours. Also, he thought derivatives were "phantom assets," whereas we had many programs that relied on derivatives. To demonstrate his view on derivatives, he immediately eliminated Kodak's corporate foreign exchange department. Harry soon brought in a new and extremely competent treasurer from IBM, Jesse Greene, and assigned Jesse as almost his first task to eliminate all derivatives from the corporation's balance sheet.

To place Harry's concern in the context of the times, a number of institutional funds in recent years had sustained major losses as a result of their managers getting carried away with the use of derivatives, and Harry was understandably frightened of KRIP suffering a black hole.

A One-Time Review by Ibbotson

Harry, as the chairman of KRIPCO, then asked Jesse to get a good outside consultant to make a fresh total review of KRIP's investment program. Jesse and I visited a couple of consultants and selected the esteemed Ibbotson Associates in Chicago to do a one-time analysis. Ibbotson submitted its 236-page report in May 1995 and included the following in its summary:

> It appears that all levels of management at Eastman Kodak are fulfilling their fiduciary responsibility and meeting the standards of the "prudent expert" rule.... [KRIP's fund also] has more asset classes, more managers, and more complexity than its peers, and is managed by one of the smallest pension staffs in corporate America... which compensates for leanness with the highest level of efficiency, competency, and commitment.

At the time, we had close to 90 different managers and 130 different investment programs.[16]

Ibbotson sustained KRIP's use of "international diversification," "alternative asset classes," and its "long-term view on investing." Ibbotson's recommendations included a greater allocation to fixed income, further improved controls on the use of derivatives, and the termination of unfunded "derivative programs for yield enhancement." Ibbotson referred specifically to our overlay programs—of commodity futures, foreign exchange, and the two overlay programs recently begun by Bridgewater. Ibbotson's report said that these programs, since their inception in 1986, had added return to KRIP and actually lowered its volatility (which means the programs must have had a negative correlation with the rest of KRIP's investments), but Ibbotson still maintained that such overlay programs were inappropriate for a pension fund. Ibbotson never elaborated as to why.

The Demise of KRIP's Overlay Programs

Immediately thereafter Harry Kavetas asked Jesse Greene to draw up a proposal for presentation to CEO George Fisher to terminate those programs. When Harry and Jesse went to see George, Harry surprisingly invited me to go along. After Jesse completed his presentation about the terminations, I said, "George, I would like, if I may, to make an alternative proposal."

George Fisher sat back in his chair, smiled, and said, "Well, it's always nice to have alternative proposals."

I proceeded with my arguments to retain these overlay programs but to institute a series of controls that I agreed made a lot of sense. Guess what happened? My idea of making an alternative proposal had been naïve. Of course, George endorsed his CFO's recommendation.

---

16. If someone in 1980 had told me we would some day have that many managers and different investment programs, I'd have thought the person was out of his mind. But as we acquired them little by little, we believed they all added value, and our well-organized monitoring procedures enabled us to supervise them effectively.

   We still had nearly 90 managers by the year 2000, and by then there were also some 110 managers who were no longer managing KRIP assets. From 1985 through 2000 we terminated, on average, about half a dozen managers per year.

It was then my sad duty to visit each of our overlay managers and tell them that their programs were being terminated, even though they had done a good job through the years. We probably should have been relieved that Harry didn't mandate the demise of all of our other programs that involved the use of derivatives.

A Review of KRIP's Legal Practices

We also hired the Washington law firm of Sutherland, Asbill & Brennan to analyze KRIP's legal positions and procedures. Sutherland's Warren Davis made a thorough review and was generally supportive of KRIP's legal practices but recommended that KRIPCO cap the potential legal liability of investment programs that utilize derivatives. As a result, with the help of our ERISA lawyer, Greg Gumina, we took several actions:

- To prevent any one manager from losing more than the assets in his account and creating a black hole in KRIP's deep pockets, we established a separate Delaware limited liability trust for each investment program authorized to use derivatives. That meant two dozen separate trusts. These separate trusts did not alter the monthly reporting package we received from our master trustee, the Boston Safe arm of Mellon Trust.

- In our management agreement with each manager who was authorized to use derivatives, we defined the kinds of derivatives he or she was authorized to use, and the maximum amount of each derivative. We set those limits after asking each manager what kinds of derivatives he would like to be able to use, why, and what limits would make sense to him.

- We got our master trustee to conduct a daily audit of the derivatives used by each of our managers and to give us a call if any manager ever exceeded his authority. We didn't expect to receive any such calls, and essentially we did not.

Changes in Staff and in KRIPCO

Another change came with the new management. Harry Kavetas was concerned about a pension staff as thin as five people—two middle management executives, one very competent professional (Kathleen Emert) who functioned as our administrative manager, and two clerical persons. Our staff carried responsibility for the $7 billion pension plan *plus* another $5 billion in 401(k) assets and $2 billion in the pension investments of some 20 of Kodak's non-U.S. subsidiaries. As a result we hired another "middle management" person—Kathleen (Kat) Mandel. Kat had previously held an executive position with the Mobil Oil pension fund. Kat helped us hire two outstanding managers—Morgan Stanley's London-based team in international stocks, and Capital International in emerging markets stocks. Kat left in 1998 and was succeeded by Dave McNiff, who for the prior 10 years had been director of pension investments at GenCorp in Akron.

Through the years, the membership on KRIPCO had evolved slowly, and as a result of the KRIPCO conferences, committee members maintained a solid understanding of agreed-upon investment strategy. As a result, the committee approved more than 95% of staff recommendations.

The nature of the committee changed when Harry Kavetas became CFO of Kodak and chairman of KRIPCO. During 1994 Bob Spooner and I discovered an investment firm comprised of a couple dozen diverse arbitrage managers of remarkable talent. Its fund had achieved net performance of about 15% per year with very little variation over a period of years. We thought we had struck gold and recommended the fund to KRIPCO. At that meeting Harry talked on and on about the dangers of derivatives and finally asked Bob and me to leave the room. When we returned we were told that the recommendation had been unanimously rejected.

We were so highly impressed by the controls instituted by the manager of the fund that we got treasurer Jesse Greene to visit the manager. Then we made the recommendation a second time, this time emphasizing all of the manager's controls. Result: Exactly what happened the first time. We were beginning to understand it was a new ball game. Incidentally, these were the only occasions when staff was asked to leave a KRIPCO meeting except when the venture capital proposal was being considered in 1983.

The defeat didn't deter Bob and me from continuing to recommend new opportunities, including illiquid ones like real estate and private corporate investments. Such recommendations usually elicited a lecture from Harry about his concerns regarding alternative investments, but then the recommendations would usually be approved. We hired a range of additional market neutral arbitrage managers, and in 1998 we convinced KRIPCO to expand its market neutral allocation to 10% of the portfolio.

In March 1999, shortly after Dave McNiff joined our staff, I took Dave to meet Harry Kavetas. Harry began the conversation by saying, "I want you to know that there are no two people who have more opposite ideas about how to manage a pension fund than Rusty and I!" Tragically, Harry died of a sudden heart attack one month later.

Performance of KRIP in the 1990s

As a result of Kodak's continuing downsizing as well as the company's 1991 decision to allow retirees to take their pensions as a lump sum, payouts from KRIP to retirees became huge, averaging each year some 11½% of the fund's market value. To raise the cash for these payouts, we followed a just-in-time approach. Each quarter we told managers in overweighted asset classes (those which had recently outperformed other asset classes) to sell the amount of assets needed for the payouts. In this way we continuously rebalanced our portfolio toward our target asset allocation. These monster payouts did not seem to dampen performance.

KRIP's performance for the five years through 1996 was among the best of its peers. But members of KRIPCO and the finance committee of the board of directors were challenged to maintain their confidence in our investment strategy in 1997 and 1998 when KRIP's return of 11% per year over those two years was the lowest recorded by any of the pension funds we considered peers. Those were the years when there was only one great place to invest—large U.S. growth stocks. Small stocks, non U.S. stocks, especially emerging markets stocks, and most private assets provided results ranging from mediocre to terrible. Any degree of diversification was penalized in those years, and our portfolio was perhaps more diversified than any other pension fund.

The market changed in 1999, and after KRIP returned 30% that year, our three-year return over 1997–99 comfortably exceeded that of the average pension fund, as measured by the TUCS median.[17] For the 10 years 1990-99, KRIP's return was over 1% per year more than the average U.S. pension fund, according to TUCS figures.

17.　The Trust Universe Comparison Service, whose universe of pension funds included some 200 master trusts.

Chapter 5

The Turn of the Century

An **Asset/Liability Study.** Throughout the 1990s, our tool to help us with asset allocation was an Efficient Frontier computer model[18] that defined volatility as the annual fluctuation of the market value of our portfolio. We knew that a better approach is an asset/liability study, which also uses an Efficient Frontier but defines volatility as the fluctuation in the pension plan's *funding ratio* or the present value of all future contributions by the plan sponsor. The funding ratio is the ratio of the market value of the plan's assets to the present value of the plan's liabilities. An asset/liability study, however, is far more complex and costly, and we postponed doing it until 1999.

We talked with five providers of asset/liability studies and selected Towers, Perrin, because its model could handle more asset classes than the others—18 of them. We were convinced that the larger the number of diverse asset classes we used, the higher we could push the Efficient Frontier. The 18 asset classes we used were as follows:

Common Stock	Fixed Income	Alternative
Kodak stock[19]	Traditional U.S. Bonds	Venture real estate
U.S. large stocks	Long U.S. bonds	Timber
U.S. small stocks	25-year zeros	Private energy
REITs	Inflation-linked bonds	Venture capital
Non-U.S. stocks	U.S. high-yield bonds	Distressed securities
Emerging markets stocks	Emerging markets debt	Market neutral

We would have liked to add several other asset classes if the computer program had been able to handle more than 18—for example, non-U.S. small stocks and components of "venture capital," including start-up

---

18.   This is a computer program that calculates asset allocations that will provide the highest possible expected return at every given level of volatility.

19.   KRIPCO continued to hold Kodak stock in its portfolio until 2003.

venture capital and other private corporate investments in the U.S. and abroad.

Our actuary, Towers, Perrin, already had complete data on our employees and retirees, so it could accurately project the plan's liabilities. The projection of asset returns, however, is totally dependent on the assumptions that are used, so we used multiple sets of varied assumptions. The matrix of correlations is especially complex. It is easy to write down different correlation assumptions but difficult to model, as most sets of correlations are mutually incompatible. If they're mathematically impossible, the model will reject them. We used two sets of correlations—Towers' assumptions, and our own. Then we used multiple sets of expected return and volatility assumptions.

For each set of assumptions, Towers used a Monte Carlo approach to calculate 500 sets of returns for each future year. True to life, everything was a probability. The model calculated the particular asset allocations that formed the "Efficient Frontier"—the *most efficient* asset allocations. For those asset allocations and any other asset allocation we wanted to try, we could compare

a) the probability distributions of future funding ratios,
b) the probability distribution of expected present values of all future company contributions to the pension fund, and
c) the likelihood of any unexpectedly large contribution that would be required in a given year.

The output was enormous. Our effort was to select a target allocation that would hold up reasonably well under all sets of assumptions and under all definitions of volatility. Notably, no matter what assumptions we used, the output of all the runs ignored traditional U.S. bonds. All the runs loved 25-year zero-coupon bonds (we called them "Zeros"), even though Zeros are extremely volatile. Zeros, however, *hedge* a pension plan's liabilities. Because the most important assumption needed to calculate the present value of liabilities is the interest assumption, and because Financial Accounting Standards require the interest assumption to vary with interest rates from year to year, the present value of liabilities also has great but parallel volatility. The average duration of KRIP's liabilities was about 10 years, so the volatility of its liabilities could be hedged with a far smaller allocation to Zeros than to shorter-term bonds.

Revised Investment Policy

The result of this effort was a revised investment policy that was approved by KRIPCO in January, 2000. The key portion of the policy statement,[20] which sets the target allocation and the benchmark portfolio, is as follows:

> **Aggregate Performance Objective.**
> Over intervals of five years and longer, to exceed the performance of a Benchmark Portfolio (rebalanced quarterly) that is invested in:
> - the remaining shares of Kodak stock in the portfolio.
> - the quarter-ending stated value of KRIP's illiquid assets (targeted not to exceed 22% of total KRIP assets).
> - 25-year zero-coupon Treasury bonds [Zeros], with performance assumed to be that of an equivalent futures portfolio, and targeted to equal a continuing 15% of total KRIP assets.

The balance of the Benchmark Portfolio shall be allocated among liquid assets with benchmarks as follows:

27.5%	Russell 1000 Index (large U.S. stocks)
16.0	Russell 2000 Index (small U.S. stocks)
3.0	NAREIT Index (real estate investment trusts)
20.0	MSCI EAFE Extended Index (non-U.S. stocks, developed economies)
14.0	MSCI Emerging Markets Free stock index
3.5	Chase High-Yield Developed Markets Index
4.5	J.P.Morgan Emerging Markets Bond Index Plus
4.5	Lehman Brothers Inflation Linked Treasury Index
7.0	Treasury bills plus 4% (absolute return programs)
100.0%	

---

20.   The entire policy statement is included as Appendix 1.

We did not target allocations to specific illiquid asset classes, such as private equity, real estate, timberland, and private energy properties. Our policy stated instead that "each new illiquid investment should be selected on an opportunistic basis so as to improve the overall portfolio's diversification and enhance its return." For purposes of the asset/liability study, however, we assumed an illiquid allocation such as the following:

10.0%	Private equity (includes venture capital and distressed securities)
7.5	Venture real estate
2.5	Timberland
2.0	Private energy properties
22.0%	

As assumptions, we entered our estimate of the *underlying* volatility of each illiquid asset class, not *reported* volatility, which is a lot lower because such a large portion of illiquid assets is reported at or close to book value.

If you look individually at the asset classes that compose KRIP's target allocation, they appear to be extremely volatile—a weighted-average expected volatility of 21% per year. But because of the relatively low correlation among many of these asset classes, the expected volatility of the overall portfolio was only about 12.5% per year. Some may still consider that a relatively high *market value volatility*. But the expected volatility of the pension plan's *funding ratio* was much lower than that, largely because of the allocation to 25-year Zeros.

By early 2000 KRIPCO had completed all changes in its portfolio to conform with its revised investment policy.

Changes in the Staff

I retired in June 2000, but left the staff with two senior executives—Bob Spooner and Dave McNiff—whom I considered among the best of all corporate pension investment directors. For whatever reason, Kodak didn't appoint either to succeed me, and in January 2003 Kodak hired John Lane as director of pension investments. Lane had previously headed the staff for Pennsylvania's public pension plans. Bob Spooner retired from Kodak later in 2002,[21] and Dave McNiff left in 2003.[22]

Performance

KRIP's asset allocation decided in January 2000 remained essentially intact over at least the next three years. During those three years, when the S&P 500 and Wilshire 5000 plummeted a total of some 38%, KRIP's portfolio achieved a slightly positive return.

Over the 10 years 1993-2002, despite its poor relative results in 1997-98, KRIP's annual rate of return of 10.8% was better than 97% of U.S. corporate pension funds,[23] some 2% per year better than the average. The standard deviation of KRIP's annual returns for those 10 years was below 11%, somewhat modest considering the turbulent stock market during those years.

And KRIP, under the leadership of John Lane, continued strong in 2003 with a return upwards of 26%, followed by a strong double-digit return in 2004. Still no new company contributions were needed by the plan.

Funding ratios—the ratio of pension assets to projected pension liabilities—dropped sharply for all pension funds in the first few years of the new century, as declining interest rates inflated the present value of liabilities. At the end of 2003, however, Kodak reported that KRIP assets equaled 99% of its liabilities, placing Kodak among the nation's best-funded corporate pension plans,[24] and KRIP's funding ratio became strong yet by the end of 2004.

The annual rates of return for Kodak's pension Trust Fund for all intervals from 1961 through 2003 are included as Appendix 2. The annual rate of return for the full 43 years 1961–2003 was 9.6%—or 5.1% real (net of inflation).

---

21. Bob became chief investment officer of the Market Street Trust Company in Corning, N.Y., which serves the financial needs of high net worth clients and families.
22. Dave joined Cornell University's investment staff, which is responsible for investing Cornell's endowment fund.
23. Based on TUCS data.
24. According to *Future Metrics*.

Appendix 1

Investment Policy Statement for Kodak's Pension Fund as Revised in January 2000[25]

Aggregate Performance Objective.

Over intervals of five years and longer, to exceed the performance of a Benchmark Portfolio (rebalanced quarterly) that is invested in:

- the remaining shares of Kodak stock in the portfolio.
- the quarter-ending stated value of KRIP's illiquid assets (which are targeted not to exceed 22% of total KRIP assets).
- 25-year zero-coupon Treasury bonds, with performance assumed to be that of an equivalent futures portfolio, and targeted to equal a continuing 15% of total KRIP assets.

The balance of the Benchmark Portfolio shall be allocated among liquid assets with benchmarks as follows:

27.5%	Russell 1000 Index (large U.S. stocks)
16.0	Russell 2000 Index (small U.S. stocks)
3.0	NAREIT Index (real estate investment trusts)
20.0	MSCI EAFE Extended Index (non-U.S. stocks, developed economies)
14.0	MSCI Emerging Markets Free stock index
3.5	Chase High-Yield Developed Markets Index
4.5	J.P.Morgan Emerging Markets Bond Index Plus
4.5	Lehman Brothers Inflation Linked Treasury Index
7.0	Treasury bills plus 4% (absolute return programs)
100.0%	

As 25-year zeros become overweighted or underweighted because of market movements, they are to be regularly rebalanced to their target. Aggregate over- or underweights in Kodak stock and illiquid assets are

---

25. I have made a small number of minor edits in this policy statement, all for the purpose of clarification without in any way altering the substance.

to be offset by adjusting the allocation to all other asset classes (except 25-year zeros) proportionately.

Aggregate Volatility.

To experience volatility of KRIP's overall plan assets (as measured by the annualized standard deviation of their returns over the latest five years) that is not materially greater than that of the Benchmark Portfolio.

Asset Allocation.

In order to hedge the present value of its pension liabilities, KRIPCO targets the continuing 15% of KRIP assets in 25-year Zeros or the equivalent. For the balance of its portfolio, KRIPCO targets a broadly diversified portfolio of asset classes that have materially higher expected returns and have relatively low correlation with one another. This target allocation is reflected in the above Benchmark Portfolio.

A portion of the Benchmark Portfolio asset class exposure is to be achieved by the use of common stock index futures and interest rate futures. Most of the cash underlying these futures is to be invested in a diversified portfolio of absolute return programs (to be known as the Portable Alpha Pool) whose aggregate results are intended to

- provide returns in excess of T-bill returns (which are required by futures managers in order to equal their index benchmark returns), and
- avoid adding materially higher volatility to KRIP's aggregate portfolio.

This Portable Alpha Pool is intended to serve as a portable alpha to certain asset classes included in the Benchmark Portfolio—mainly large-cap U.S. stocks...and Zeros—and will total up to 25% of total KRIP assets.

If the allocation to any liquid asset class should at any time vary by more than 3% from its target, the Pension Investments staff is to re-allocate assets in such a way as to bring that allocation within 3% of its Benchmark allocation. Within this band, the Pension Investments staff will decide how to raise needed cash or to apply company contributions.

Liquid Assets.

"Liquid assets" include any investments KRIPCO can readily convert to cash within a year. These consist of stock, fixed income securities, and arbitrage investments, including derivatives (such as options, futures on the stock and bond markets, and foreign exchange forward contracts).

KRIPCO should consider investments in *all* liquid asset classes and should base its portfolio weight in each class at any particular time on whatever combination it expects will provide optimal risk/volatility characteristics for the aggregate portfolio relative to the present value of KRIP's projected liabilities. KRIPCO should also seek diversification within asset classes. For example, in common stocks, KRIPCO should normally seek to have managers that have different styles, ones that focus on different sizes of stocks and different geographic orientations in the world. KRIPCO may therefore hire multiple specialist managers in a single asset class.

Derivative securities can be very useful in a pension account as a means to reduce risk or to facilitate asset allocation. If misused, however, derivatives can create unexpected risks. Hence, each *separate* KRIP account that uses derivatives should be maintained in an individual limited liability trust. And for each such account a definition of allowable derivatives and an exposure limit to those derivatives should be developed with the manager for that account. Where feasible, there should also be an independent mechanism to create a timely flag if that manager should ever invest in excluded derivatives or exceed its exposure limit.

Because short-term fixed income securities are the lowest-return asset class over any long-term interval, KRIPCO should target its holdings of these securities at the lowest possible level commensurate with benefit payouts and other cash needs for its investment programs. In general, all short-term fixed income investments other than those held for market timing purposes (if any) should be "equitized" through a diversity of overlay programs.

Illiquid Assets.

"Illiquid assets" include any investment that KRIPCO cannot readily choose to convert to cash within a year. These assets are usually private investments, grouped under three main categories:

- Real estate
- Corporate ventures
- Natural resources

Each new illiquid investment should be selected on an opportunistic basis so as to improve the overall portfolio's diversification and enhance its return.

For purposes of administrative efficiency, no individual commitment to an illiquid investment should normally be made for less than 0.3% of total KRIP assets. Nor should such a commitment normally be made for much more than 0.5%. Such commitments are much smaller than typical commitments to managers of liquid assets. This is because a great diversity of asset classes and managers, including time diversification, is desirable due to the illiquid and often specialized nature of private investments.

The success of KRIP's illiquid investment program will depend on the extent that over time KRIP's aggregate illiquid investments either a) exceed returns on the Russell 3000 Index by 3% per year or b) achieve a net IRR of 15% per year.

Manager Selection and Retention.

To achieve superior investment returns with average or below-average volatility, KRIPCO should continuously seek investment managers and investment opportunities that have expected rates of return higher than those expected from existing salable assets, especially if this would maintain the aggregate volatility and facilitate the manageability of KRIP's overall portfolio.

KRIPCO's goal is to have its investments in every asset class managed by the world's best investors in that asset class. Until such time (if ever) that the Kodak pension investment staff can prove itself world class in managing any particular asset class, the day-to-day portfolio management of all KRIP investments shall be performed outside the company.

All managers—both prospective and existing—should be evaluated under five criteria:

- *Character*—Integrity, reliability, worthy of our trust.
- *Expected return*—Historic return overlaid by an evaluation of the predictive value of that historic return as well as other factors that may seem relevant in that instance and may have predictive value.
- *Expected impact on overall KRIP volatility relative to the present value of KRIP liabilities*—This evaluation has two facets:
  - *The expected volatility of the manager's investments*—the historic volatility of his investments overlaid by an evaluation of the predictive value of that historic volatility, as well as a recognition of the historic volatility of that manager's asset class in general.
  - *The expected correlation*—of the manager's volatility with that of KRIP's other assets and with the present value of KRIP's liabilities.
- *Liquidity*—How readily in the future can the account be converted to cash, and how satisfactory is that in relation to KRIP's overall portfolio?
- *Legal/prudence issues*—Is there any legal concern? After considering the above four criteria, is the selection or retention of the manager appropriate under ERISA's rules of fiduciary responsibility?

Net Annual Rates of Return on Eastman Kodak Company Pension Trust Fund, 1961–2003

To End of	'61	'62	'63	'64	'65	'66	'67	'68	'69	'70	'71	'72	'73	'74	'75	'76	'77	'78	'79	'80
'03	10	9	10	10	10	10	10	10	10	10	11	10	10	11	13	12	12	13	13	13
'02	9	9	10	9	9	9	10	9	9	10	10	10	10	11	12	12	12	13	13	13
'01	9	9	10	10	10	9	10	10	10	10	11	10	10	11	13	13	12	13	14	13
'00	10	10	10	10	10	10	10	10	10	11	11	11	11	12	14	13	13	14	14	14
'99	10	10	11	10	10	10	11	10	10	11	11	11	11	12	14	14	13	15	15	15
'98	9	9	10	10	10	9	10	10	10	10	11	10	10	11	13	13	13	14	14	14
'97	10	9	10	10	10	10	10	10	10	10	11	11	10	12	14	13	13	14	15	14
'96	9	9	10	10	10	9	10	9	10	10	11	10	10	12	14	13	13	14	14	14
'95	9	9	10	9	9	9	10	9	9	10	10	10	10	11	13	13	13	14	14	14
'94	9	9	9	9	9	9	9	9	9	9	10	10	9	11	13	13	12	14	14	14
'93	9	9	10	9	9	9	10	9	9	10	11	10	10	11	14	13	13	15	15	15
'92	9	9	9	9	9	9	9	9	9	9	10	10	9	11	13	13	13	15	15	14
'91	9	9	9	9	9	9	9	9	9	9	10	10	9	11	14	13	13	15	15	15
'90	8	8	9	9	8	8	9	8	8	9	10	9	8	10	13	12	12	14	14	14
'89	9	9	9	9	9	9	9	9	9	9	10	10	9	11	14	14	14	16	16	16
'88	8	8	9	9	8	8	9	8	8	9	10	9	9	11	14	13	13	15	16	15
'87	8	8	9	8	8	8	8	8	8	8	9	9	8	10	14	13	13	15	16	15
'86	8	8	9	8	8	8	9	8	8	8	10	9	8	11	14	13	13	16	17	17
'85	8	8	9	8	8	7	8	7	8	8	9	8	8	10	14	13	13	16	17	17
'84	7	7	8	7	7	6	7	6	6	7	8	7	6	9	13	12	11	14	15	15
'83	7	7	8	7	7	7	7	6	7	7	8	7	6	9	14	13	12	16	18	17
'82	7	6	7	7	6	6	7	5	6	6	7	6	5	8	13	12	11	15	17	16
'81	6	5	7	6	5	5	6	4	4	5	6	5	3	6	12	10	9	13	15	13
'80	6	6	7	6	6	5	6	5	5	6	7	5	4	8	15	13	12	19	25	32
'79	5	5	6	5	4	4	5	3	3	3	4	3	0	4	12	8	6	13	20	
'78	4	4	5	4	3	3	3	2	1	2	3	0	-3	1	10	5	-0	8		
'77	4	4	5	4	3	2	3	1	1	1	2	-1	-5	-0	10	3	-8			
'76	5	4	6	5	4	3	4	2	2	2	4	0	-4	2	20	15				
'75	4	4	5	4	3	2	3	0	-0	-0	2	-3	-9	-4	26					
'74	3	2	4	2	1	-0	0	-3	-4	-4	-4	-11	-23	-26						
'73	6	5	7	6	5	3	5	2	1	2	5	-2	-20							
'72	8	7	10	9	8	7	10	7	7	10	20	19								
'71	7	6	9	8	7	5	8	4	4	6	21									
'70	6	5	7	6	4	2	5	-1	-4	-7										
'69	7	6	10	8	7	5	9	2	-1											
'68	8	8	12	10	9	7	15	5												
'67	9	8	13	11	11	8	26													
'66	6	5	10	7	4	-7														
'65	9	8	16	14	16															
'64	8	5	17	13																
'63	6	2	21																	
'62	-1	-15																		
'61	15																			

'81	'82	'83	'84	'85	'86	'87	'88	'89	'90	'91	'92	'93	'94	'95	'96	'97	'98	'99	'00	'01	'02	'03
12	13	13	12	13	12	12	12	12	11	13	12	12	11	12	12	11	10	11	6	7	12	26
12	13	12	12	12	11	11	11	11	10	12	10	11	10	11	10	8	7	7	1	-2	0	
12	13	13	12	13	12	12	12	12	11	13	12	12	11	12	11	10	9	10	1	-4		
13	14	14	13	14	13	13	14	13	13	15	13	14	13	15	15	14	13	17	6			
14	15	14	14	15	14	14	14	14	13	16	14	16	14	17	17	17	17	30				
13	14	13	13	14	13	12	13	12	12	14	12	13	11	14	13	11	5					
13	15	14	13	14	13	13	14	13	12	15	13	15	13	17	17	16						
13	14	14	13	14	13	13	14	13	12	15	13	15	12	18	18							
13	14	14	13	14	12	12	13	12	11	14	12	14	9	19								
13	14	13	12	13	12	11	12	11	10	13	10	11	1									
14	15	14	14	15	13	13	14	13	12	18	14	23										
13	14	14	13	14	12	11	13	11	8	16	6											
13	15	14	14	15	13	12	14	13	9	26												
12	14	13	12	13	10	9	11	7	-5													
14	17	16	15	17	15	15	19	20														
14	16	15	14	17	13	12	18															
13	16	15	13	16	10	6																
14	18	17	15	21	15																	
14	19	18	16	29																		
11	16	12	4																			
13	22	22																				
9	22																					
-3																						

Intervals of negative annual returns

The hypotenuse shows the fund's return for each individual year.

Each number in the triangle is the fund's compound annual rate of return for the respective interval of years.

Index

Colophon

Design & Production
Amelia Hugill-Fontanel
Marnie Soom

Typefaces
Adobe Minion Pro
Adobe Myriad Pro

Printing
Lulu.com